THE DECLUTTER CODE

10 Simple Steps to Clarity

YVETTE BOWLIN

DECLUTTERED PRESS

Published in the United States by Decluttered Press

For information about special discounts on bulk purchases,
please visit decluttercode.com/bulk

For information on speeches, courses and workshops with the author,
please inquire at yvettebowlin.com

Library of Congress Control Number
2015921350

ISBN-10: 0-692-60299-2 (paperback)
ISBN-13: 978-0-692-60299-7 (paperback)

Manufactured in the United States of America

Cover design by Yvette Bowlin and Anna Nosach

For you.

TABLE OF CONTENTS

If

RUDYARD KIPLING

If you can keep your head when all about you
  Are losing theirs and blaming it on you,
If you can trust yourself when all men doubt you,
  But make allowance for their doubting too;
If you can wait and not be tired by waiting,
  Or being lied about, don't deal in lies,
Or being hated, don't give way to hating,
  And yet don't look too good, nor talk too wise:

If you can dream—and not make dreams your master;
  If you can think—and not make thoughts your aim;
If you can meet with Triumph and Disaster
  And treat those two impostors just the same;
If you can bear to hear the truth you've spoken
  Twisted by knaves to make a trap for fools,
Or watch the things you gave your life to, broken,
  And stoop and build 'em up with worn-out tools:

If you can make one heap of all your winnings
  And risk it on one turn of pitch-and-toss,
And lose, and start again at your beginnings
  And never breathe a word about your loss;
If you can force your heart and nerve and sinew
  To serve your turn long after they are gone,
And so hold on when there is nothing in you
  Except the Will which says to them: 'Hold on!'

If you can talk with crowds and keep your virtue,
  Or walk with Kings—nor lose the common touch,
If neither foes nor loving friends can hurt you,
  If all men count with you, but none too much;
If you can fill the unforgiving minute
  With sixty seconds' worth of distance run,
Yours is the Earth and everything that's in it,
  And—which is more—you'll be a Man, my son!

PROLOGUE

You might want to put this book down if you're expecting organization tips and closet-clearing advice. This wouldn't be for you. You won't find tips to organize your desk or clever ways to display your accessories addiction. If all you're looking to gain from these pages is a way to organize your clutter, this book won't help.

Instead, this book is designed to enlighten you to the reasons *why* you have a cluttered desk and way too many accessories. I plan to expose you to the truth *underneath* your clutter and how to clean up *that* mess. That's the good news.

If your house is in disarray and you can't seem to get it under control, this book is for you.

If your relationships are suffering from poor communication and discord, this book is for you.

If weight loss eludes you no matter what diet or exercise routine you try, this book is for you.

If "I'm broke" is your favorite thing to say to your friends and family, this book is for you.

If you're an artist and you hit creative blocks when you're trying to get your best work out there, this book is for you.

If you're a yogi striving to maintain the peace you get on your mat and carry it with you off your mat, this book is for you.

If you love saying Yes to new projects and adding more stuff to your plate, even though you're constantly spread too thin, this book is for you.

If you're a business owner held hostage by your business and its nonstop workload, this book is for you.

And for all my fellow Type A personalities, if you're looking for ways to fire your inner control freak, this book is for you.

If you kept on reading, my guess is you have an inkling that clutter stems much deeper than a closet or a drawer. Yet we still catch ourselves looking for an external answer to an internal situation, like a drug addict looking for a quick high to cure his lows. We've been emptying drawers and donating clothes hoping for, finally, the way out of clutter. We've been using superficial, tangible methods to clean up deep, intangible disorder.

Contrary to what we've been taught, to clear clutter we have to start from the inside out.

On these pages, I'll take you through the steps of the Declutter Code and you'll learn how to declutter your life. I've been through the process myself (and still practicing), so I can vouch for the results. I can happily say my hoarding (clinging, collecting, amassing and storing) tendencies have dramatically been curbed. And if you know me, that's saying a lot. In this book, you'll hear my story and the nuggets of wisdom I've learned on my journey of clearing the clutter.

I should mention, I'm no doctor, biologist, neurologist, or anything of the sort. There's no hypnosis or NLP incorporated on these pages. None of that is necessary. This book contains advice for those who've been where I've been and want to be free of clutter—namely its predecessors, anxiety and overwhelm.

The Declutter Code isn't science. It's not tested on rats. It's not governmental law or principled like a constitution. It's not a list of rules. There are no penalties for mistakes. And actually, you can't make a mistake here because there is no right or wrong in the Code.

It doesn't cost you anything to get started. Rather, it might *save* you from wasting any more money. It doesn't require a college degree to understand. It's so simple, your kids can follow along. It doesn't involve an overseas trip to implement. You can do this right where you are, right now.

The Declutter Code only requires your willingness to try.

This book presents tips and techniques on how to start living a fuller, freer life. If that sounds like a worthy cause, keep reading.

This book is for *you*. Apply the philosophy wherever it fits. Take what resonates with you into your life, and leave what doesn't on these pages.

As a gift of encouragement, beyond this book there are resources and a community available to support and encourage you as you begin to clear clutter from your life. Visit decluttercode.com to join me and my network of friends as we declutter together. Save yourself years of disappointing results running from room to room picking up junk and thousands of dollars buying the latest space-saver craze—when that's barely scratching the surface.

Let's get to the root of the clutter.

INTRODUCTION

We've got messy minds. Overcrowded, overloaded and overwhelmed minds. It's no wonder we're overthinking and overanalyzing as we finger-swipe in and out of three different social media networks at once, texting back and forth with friends, all while listening to podcasts. And it's no surprise we feel overbooked as we take business phone calls and fill our calendars with meetings and work events, one after the other.

Messy minds lead to messy lives.

Naturally it would happen this way: messy mind, messy life. Our minds don't shut off and neither does the noise around us. We let anything in that wants to get in. The TV's on, the radio's blaring, the phone's pinging with every new text, and email's open 24/7. Information is so readily accessible, it's easy to get wrapped up in having to know it all. And after knowing it all, we try to do it all. An endless cycle that can go on forever like a hamster running on a wheel or a dog chasing its tail.

We're split and scattered between past, present and future, juggling roles and responsibilities. We're caught up in regrets about yesterday and worries about tomorrow. We hit overwhelm and we crash.

Peace and presence drift away. We lose clarity.

Clutter's not an external problem just like overwhelm is not an external problem. Clutter in any form starts in your head. The filthy house? In your head. The disorganized office? In your head. The unhealthy body? In your head. The chaotic relationship? In your head.

If we're frantic and crazed inside, evidence is bound to show up outside like an infection. **Order eludes us when we attempt to organize environmental clutter without first attending to mental clutter.**

(Throughout this text, I'll use the label, "environment" as anything outside of your internal being: your external appearance, your home, your relationships, your surroundings, your office, etc.) Junk will keep piling up in our homes and relationships if we never attend to the root of the build-up—our own mental junk. So we have to be swept clean from the inside out, taking a broom to our minds.

Now that the biggest takeaway from this book is behind us, we just have to talk specifics. This book is divided into two parts:

- Part 1 uncovers what's really causing the clutter in our lives. We dive deep into *why* we are anxious and overwhelmed.

- Part 2 introduces the Declutter Code, the ten-step plan that takes us from clutter to clarity. The Code guides us through decluttering our lives from the inside out.

Are you ready?

You want answers fast, I get it. But if you think you don't have time to read this book, you don't have time *not* to. You picked up this book for a reason. Follow that gut instinct and let this book provide some insight. Clutter will continue to swallow you if you don't take a good look at *why* it keeps piling up. If you don't rein it in, clutter will continue to take over your life.

You'll discover this book will actually return the time spent reading, in time gained living free from clutter.

–Yvette

PART 1

THE TRUTH ABOUT CLUTTER

The best way out is always through.
—ROBERT FROST

CHAPTER 1

IT'S ALL CLUTTER

What is clutter anyway? We've all seen a cluttered room, a cluttered car, a cluttered schedule and we think we know what clutter is, but our opinions all vary. Whatever we believe clutter to be is very telling as to the depth of clutter in our own lives.

Clutter is defined as a collection of things lying in an untidy mass. But Merriam-Webster only scratches the surface with that definition. Clutter pervades every nook in our lives. From the dirty socks on the floor to the latest gossip at the water cooler, it's all clutter.

Let me set the scene.

You look around the house and it's everywhere. The overflowing drawer of socks. Excessive pots and pans in the kitchen. The pile of mail on the kitchen counter. Several pairs of shoes at the front door. Outdated magazines on the coffee table. Stacks of DVDs by the TV. Unchecked honey-do lists. The kids' rooms full of toys. The shelves of dusty awards and sports memorabilia. The overgrown lawn.

It's even in our hearts as the baggage we carry from past relationships. The grief and unforgiveness. The broken promises from ex-lovers. Our broken promises to ex-lovers. The painful memories. The grudges we hold. The friendships that didn't last but still haunt us. The longing for a mate. The demands we place on spouses and children. The mourning of deceased loved ones. Our firsts. Our lasts.

It lives in our bodies as the ten pounds we can't lose no matter what crash diet we try. It's the beer bellies. The boob implants. The sicknesses, colds and flus. The injury and inflammation in our muscles and joints. The disease, the cancer, the triple bypass. The unkempt appearance. The poor hygiene. The substance abuse and drug addictions. The overeating. The not eating.

It takes over our finances. It shows up as the money problems we acquire from impatience and poor planning. The empty pockets. The depleted bank accounts. The frugality. The lack. The credit card debt. The payday loans. The fallen credit scores. The past due notices. The delinquencies. The collection calls. The bankruptcy. The poverty. The identity fraud. The excessive spending. The impulsive spending.

It shows up in business. In the way the business is run. In the absence of systems. The poor filing. The jam-packed schedules. The endless to-do lists. The poor communication between partners. The mismanagement of staff. The inability to delegate. The company morale. The subpar service with clients. The complaints. The refunds. The bad reviews.

It shows up digitally, too, as the hundreds of homeless desktop icons. The confusing folder structure and unorganized files. The documents, the spreadsheets, the databases. The web apps. The mobile apps. The prying text messages. The social media networks we visit daily. The excessive tabs open in our Internet browser waiting to be dealt with. The email inbox abyss. The unread emails. The unreplied-to emails. The spam.

With all this clutter floating around, we're overwhelmed, overloaded, overstimulated and overcommitted. Overwhelm, especially, is debilitating. It's that drowning feeling of defeat; being overcome with endless objectives and obligations so much so that we run on fumes before we completely shut down. It's confusion and anxiety, the absence of clarity and confidence. It's being so mentally overtasked we can't see straight. Our vision is blurred and our steps aren't as certain when we're overwhelmed.

How would you describe your feelings of overwhelm? Do you feel that way often? How do you usually deal with it?

Clutter is anything and everything that clouds and corrodes and cripples our lives. In short, clutter hijacks our peace. You can probably see how clutter leads to overwhelm.

Everything that is not Truth is clutter. Even our habits are clutter. And sometimes habits are the most overwhelming thing for us because it's difficult to change them when they're so deeply engrained into our psyche and way of life. Some of them we don't even know we have. Basically, habits amount to operating on auto-pilot. They blanket over our simplest, purest selves with behavior designed to make us feel safe (more on this in Chapter 10). Habits are crutches in our lives. Things that hold us back and often hold us up. While there are both habits that aid a healthy lifestyle and habits that diminish it, overall, habits themselves and their respective triggers are clutter because they are mindless substitutes for presence.

What's important to note is habits promote and perpetuate the state of mind from which they were created. Binge eating, mindless. Healthy eating, mindful. So the recommended thing to do is build habits from a present, awakened place. If, after reading this book, you're inspired to form new habits, the Declutter Code will help you cultivate a decluttered, conscious state of mind that serves to birth a decluttered, conscious way of life.

Hopefully this encourages your desire to clear away clutter in order to restore balance and peace in your life. If you can't get a handle on your cluttered life or you're asking yourself, "Why even bother trying to clean clutter because it doesn't ever seem to go away," continue reading and open yourself up to the process. With the Declutter Code, we begin to take stock of our clutter and recognize its origin. This level of awareness begins our cleansing transformation.

CHAPTER 2

THE BATTLE WITH STUFF

I wasn't always as tidy as my life looks now. I had so much "stuff" growing up, through college and as I started my career. It all just sort of latched onto me and I let it all stay. Clothes, shoes, accessories. Travel souvenirs. CDs, DVDs. Notebooks, pencils, pens. My treasure trove of buttons, rocks and old keys. As is typical of an expressive personality, all of these collections were things I was proud of.

What a mess.

Turns out, we are all naturally inclined to live simply, we just don't always have the awareness to do so. I personally didn't know how to ignore the temptation to acquire stuff or tune into the small voice inside saying, "Stop. Enough already." Stop collecting, stop buying, stop hoarding. That instinct was always there, talking to me. That inner voice that knew I didn't need all that stuff spoke very clearly—I just wasn't listening.

That small voice knows how to keep clutter at bay and clear the clutter that's already collected. It has the same simple message on repeat over and over. The same answer all the time.

One day I listened to it. It told me that clutter was born from the trash in my head and the ringmaster of this clutter circus was my own thoughts. It told me that I couldn't be defined by all this stuff, that who I was couldn't be found in what I owned.

I heard this and everything changed. I saw through the stuff, and found *me*. Up until that point, I hadn't been cleaning my clutter efficiently. I was still shopping all the time, adorning this "person" I had created. Collecting. Showcasing. I would force fit each hanger into my closet to make room for old clothes, new clothes, and "one day" clothes—you know, that dress that will one day fit your perfect body. I'd dust all my displayed trinkets to keep them shiny. I'd rearrange my bookshelves to fit my latest Amazon shipment, and then I'd alphabetize all the books. I'd even buy home decor for a house I didn't live in yet.

When it came to productivity, I'd jot notes and to-do lists on post-its, notepads and journals and have them all piled up to go back to later. Meanwhile, lists and scribbles trashed my desk, leaving barely any room for my computer keyboard. Then I'd spend hours organizing my desk before starting to work, and then run out of motivation (or the time!) to actually sit down and work. I ended up not being productive on my to-do list at all.

The day I heard the small voice, I learned that my attempts to cure my clutter "problem" were just distractions—I was treating the *symptoms* of clutter as opposed to dealing with its cause. I had been letting environmental clutter distract me from what started the mess. I let the visible clutter in the office and kitchen convince me that I only needed to donate stuff I didn't use and the problem would go away. But what about my tendency to hoard in the first place?

I was addicted to that sigh of relief after cleaning out a closet of unused clothes or a pantry of expired food. It kept me hypnotized. We all feel satisfaction after a good spring cleaning, because cleaning feels like progress. Even the process itself is encouraging. Busying ourselves with cleaning out drawers, closets and shelves has a sedative nature to it that makes time fly. Then afterward, we feel accomplished! At least we got *something* done.

There's a mindful component, too, when we're willing to part with something. Small sparks of freedom shoot off like fireworks. No wonder I was addicted to those small blasts of triumph.

But those house-cleaning sprints never stopped the next day's clutter from infiltrating my newly organized pantry shelf. My usual habits took over like invisible saboteurs. Eventually, all my usual piles of papers, packed drawers and stuffed closet racks would creep up on me again. Yet I continued to shop and store, collect and hoard. A crazy, manic cycle.

Maybe you can relate?

We all go through it, the battle with stuff. We all have our collections, those trophies we proudly display. We all have our sentimental toys, those things we can't part with. And our clutter cycle continues.

We don't realize how we crowd and complicate our own lives with the clutter we willingly usher in. Like any superhero story, if we don't uncover our clutter's weakness, we'll stay powerless against it.

The clutter I saw with my two eyes ended up being the reason I stayed cluttered. Only the items I could see and touch were getting my attention. Turns out, there was more there than a vacuum could suck up. For so long, I avoided the work I really needed to do: clear the clutter I couldn't see.

CHAPTER 3

MY INNER GARAGE SALE

You could say I had a lot of junk to wade through before finally taking a machete to the clutter in my life. Probably because I learned the art of hoarding early.

Raised in a household of seven, it was mom, dad, my four siblings and me. Mom's a shopaholic; Dad's a packrat. The motto was implicit: *you can never have too much stuff, and once you own it, you have to keep it forever.* We five kids shared one bathroom, one TV, and one Nintendo console. My two sisters and I shared one bedroom, one desk and one closet with three budding wardrobes. Shopping, storing and sharing small spaces…let's just say it quickly got out of hand.

But it was never about my upbringing.

It would take me finally living on my own to learn that only *I* could control my hoarding. It had nothing to do with my early housemates. Even in my own place, clutter followed me. Then it became plainly obvious that I was responsible for how cluttered my life became; no one else could help and no one else was to blame. Declutter duty fell solely on *my* shoulders.

Those first few attempts to hack through the clutter included *organizing* instead of *clearing*. My idea of cleaning was getting desk organizers for my papers, waterproof containers for my books, and collapsible vacuum-seal bags for my clothes. Only the best for my clutter. The reality check hit when I set out to backpack across Brazil a few years ago. I learned firsthand how to simplify my life and stop hoarding as I prepared for a seven-month long trip. I knew that everything for the trip had to fit on my back, the stuff I didn't love or need had to be purged, and what stayed home had to fit into a 5'x10' storage unit. There was exactly one month between buying my ticket to leave and my departure date. I had to move fast. That meant most of those tightly sealed containers had to go.

My biggest challenge was to stop being so sentimental. I would pull a blouse out of the closet, rehash its origin story and list all the reasons why I couldn't let it go. Everything I grabbed came attached with an energy, an emotion, and an excuse to keep it. Instead of purging, I was reminiscing! Sandy, the Cabbage Patch doll, wore some unforgettable hair-dos in Kindergarten courtesy of yours truly. My eighth grade classmates gave me hilarious birthday cards that always cracked me up. Those college courses were not only intimidating but their textbooks had information I promised myself I would reference again one day.

No way was I letting this stuff go.

Fast forward a few long, grueling days later, I tossed each of them in the trash. Took awhile, but something struck me as I sat in a sea of my past. It dawned on me that it wasn't the item itself that held any power, it was its memory. The object I held was just that, an object. So I decided to give myself five minutes of nostalgia. I relived the many afternoons playing mommy to the yarn-haired baby. I relived all the birthday parties where I'd get roasted. I even relived the agonizing hours of cramming for college exams.

I smiled as I stared behind me, feeling the memories in my heart, and then I took the stuffed and stitched fabric doll, the pieces of folded cardstock with 'Happy Birthday' scrawled all over, and the dense, outdated books and threw them in the trash.

Needing to downsize for the trip to Brazil was the main reason I was so motivated to clean house; I refused to pay rent at Public Storage to store anything I didn't need. But that didn't end up being the only reason I started rethinking everything I owned. It was what I felt as I purged the revered mementos. I felt the weight the clutter bore on me, emotionally and physically. I felt every possession that unsettled me. And, as I purged, I began to feel the freedom of detaching.

With a newfound determination to stay clear-headed about the energetic effects of my hoarding in recent years, I'm seeing *through* the clutter before it piles up. I see clutter down to its core and I'm discovering why it's here. I now notice my *need* for things, however imaginary it is.

All these years, I had been giving my stuff meaning. But I realized I don't have to. I could stop placing meaning on the things that weigh me down and keep me lost in clutter, because all I was doing was bolstering my dependency on it. Detaching from arbitrary meaning freed me to get rid of everything that didn't serve me anymore. Everything that glued me to the past. I could easily remove the stuff that kept me disconnected, disorganized and dissatisfied, if I just removed the meaning that made me keep it around.

I woke up, and I got off the hamster wheel.

By the time I was on the plane to Brazil, I'd purged nearly 60% of my possessions. What a load off, literally.

I experienced a profound freedom during my travels. Living with less actually resulted in living *more*. More freely, more abundantly, more easily. I lived so simply abroad that when I finally returned home, I was determined to maintain the minimalist lifestyle I honed in the months backpacking through Brazil. I wanted to apply simple living to my home and work life. In family and business. I couldn't go back to the way things had been before; I had seen the light.

Now I hear that inner voice, that instinct, tell me when I'm filling holes with stuff. When I'm chasing what I think I lack. All that anxiety started to go away the minute I stopped relying on material possessions to make me happy. This transformation was years in the making. I picked up helpful tips from mystics, pastors, teachers, authors, professional organizers, productivity coaches, and chiefly from my own experience. Ultimately, I found that the less I owned, acquired or borrowed, the easier life became. Or better said, the *less complicated* life became.

Wading through it all, I uncovered the key to decluttering.

It isn't just the physical act of throwing things away, or the good karma from donating old clothes, it's the way we let our feelings guide us through the process.

To declutter, we have to *feel* our way through.

CHAPTER 4

THE SIX SENSES

Feeling is our body's craft, its primary purpose and skill. Feeling is how we experience the world. It's how we experience God. And it's our only accurate measurement of Truth.

We're born with Feeling as our body's expert sensory perception. We're sentient beings, and feeling is sensing. Ostensibly, we *sense* via the work of the ears, nose, eyes, mouth and skin. However, Feeling manifests as more than just sensing cool blades of grass between your fingers, or the warmth of the sun on your face. More than just tasting the saltiness of food on your tongue or hearing the resonant sound of your own voice. It goes much deeper.

Feeling is internal work, taking place inside our core. Like that vibration we feel pulsating in our bellies when we're excited or frightened. Or that gut instinct nudging us toward a decision either beneficial or detrimental.

Feeling is also the way music moves you. The way a hug changes your physiology. The way a compliment brightens your day.

Feeling is the job of the *six* senses. Yes, six. If that number sounds like a scary movie, that's not what I mean. There's a sixth sense that's rarely acknowledged by parents or doctors, and hardly ever taught in schools or books. Unfortunately, we're not often told of this other sense. So allow me to introduce our sixth sense, the mind.

The mind is one part of the six-part sensory network. The six senses that make up this sensory network work in unison to *feel*. The mind isn't the "brain" or anything we can physically place our hands upon. It's an energy, a nonphysical powerhouse like the other five senses. And while the body is a palpable structure, the feeling it offers is truly a sensory *experience*—without much physicality to it.

Let me explain.

The body's ears, nose, eyes, mouth and skin interact with the world and deliver energetic messages (sensations) to the mind. The role of the sixth sense then is to interpret and intellectualize these sensations— thereby translating the messages into useable information. In other words, the sixth sense "makes sense" of what it receives; it imparts meaning.

The mind assigns meaning through thought—this is its sensory power.

Ears hear. Noses smell. Eyes see. Mouths taste. Hands touch. And minds *think*.

It's All in Your Head

The mind gives thought to sensation. This mental processing is known as the act of *perceiving*.

Perception relies on all six senses. Together, our six senses perceive the material world (matter) and produce a human experience. This Feeling-thought exchange is how we relate to our surroundings, determine meaning, form habits and move from Point A to Point B.

Ironically, it's not until we perceive (think) something with our mind, that we ever *hear, smell, see, taste* or *touch* it. The mind is the filter for the information we receive, the buffer between us and our life experience. Without the sixth sense, as mental perception, we don't ever come "in contact" with the world. The mind is how we *take it all in*.

We see what the mind senses. The mind determines our overall sensory experience. So even the purity of sensory messages gets manipulated by the mind, as the mind has the final say on what message was *actually* sent. Fact and fiction are both in the eye of the beholder, both equally subjective. Both subject to mind's acceptance or rejection.

The perceiving mind sets the standard for whether we relish or reject incoming messages. As a result, the sixth sense is the predominant factor affecting the quality of our life experience. That's a big deal!

It's as the old adage goes, "Perception is reality." Essentially, you could crown the mind with the task of *creating* our entire life experience. Because what we perceive is the only reality we'll ever know. **Everything we deem to be reality is so only with respect to our thoughts about it.**

What we perceive is what we come to believe; what we determine has happened, is happening and will happen. Mental perception tells us what we heard, what we smelled, what we saw, what we felt and what we tasted. And when we set our minds on something, it's rare anyone can persuade us otherwise.

In this way, perception informs our *awareness*—which is a profound level of understanding and insight. It's through awareness that things become clear, as if our inner vision improved to 20/20, sharp and crisp.

Without awareness, our view is muddled. With awareness, we have X-ray vision.

You could consider the function of the mind like an amplifier for its five counterparts within the sensory network. Favorable sensations become delight. Unfavorable sensations become dread. Through thought alone, the mind amplifies the intensity of every sound, scent, vision, flavor and texture.

Just as the mind can amplify the senses, it can also suppress them. The mind can turn off hearing, listening only to the information it wants to receive, and discarding the rest. (Selective hearing is a real thing!) The mind hears what it wants to hear, sees what it wants to see, and so on.

In this way, it can numb hands, blind eyes and mute tongues, all based on what it's choosing to take in that moment. While we're tasting, we aren't touching because the mind does not perceive both simultaneously. Test it out; pop a grape in your mouth. Feel the round shape. Bite into it; taste its flavor, feel the texture. As you do this, do you find that you are tasting the grape exactly at the same time as you are focused on its shape? Even if you tried, I bet your answer is no.

This is because we don't sense everything at once; we first smell and then taste, for instance, as the mind can only focus on and process one sensory message at a time. It might seem as though you could mentally tap in to both sensations at once, but the mind toggles one to the other faster than the blink of an eye.

Let's Get Sensual

Perception happens now, regardless of when the thought first occurs. The same mental processing goes into thinking about the past as does wondering about the future. We perceive both memory and anticipation using the entire sensory network and its Feeling-thought connection. The mind does the same job recalling the past as it does imagining the future. It calls upon the five senses to enhance the experience of recall and expectancy alike.

Let's play a little game to witness the six senses and perception in action. Close your eyes. Think back to your favorite childhood memory. If the memory involved mom baking cookies in the kitchen, can you smell them as if she just pulled them out of the oven? If the memory involved playing at the beach, can you smell the ocean air? Whatever the memory, can you remember it as vividly as if it were happening right now?

And if you shared that memory with your siblings (who were with you at the time), would they agree that your recollection was exactly how it happened? Would they include different details when giving their rendition? Was mom baking cookies, or a pie? Were you playing at the beach, or the park?

As it goes for memories is as it goes for our "real-time" life experience. All senses band together to paint a picture, while the mind guides each brush stroke. This picture, with its smells, sights and sounds, textures, tastes and thoughts, illustrates our *story*.

CHAPTER 5

OUR SENSATIONAL STORY

The six senses tell a visual, visceral story; the mind being both illustrator and author. Thought is the ink; it scribes the interpretations, definitions and explanations.

Story takes shape the second we start explaining and designating meaning to things. The mind perceives patterns (inside and out) in life to help it do the explaining, labeling everything accordingly. These labels assemble and apply meaning to what is, substantiating all of existence. They tell of cause and effect, motive and consequence. They form a library of reasons, references, reactions and recollections. Judgments, opinions, biases. Preferences, prejudices. They form mental clutter.

The labels, these *words* of our story, have power because we give them power. We give them the ability to define and explain. To tickle and entertain. To bruise and scar.

We assign labels to our Feelings—as "emotions"—and associate them with a mental state. So each word carries an energy, a vibration and a definition because once we Feel anything, we immediately attach a few letters to it to remind us later what a similar Feeling is and what it means.

In using choice words to tell our stories, we build our vocabulary, our language and, ultimately, our belief system. Yet, in trying to make sense of what is, making it applicable and useful to life, we end up making what *is* something it is *not* (nonsense). Whatever we experience *is what it is*—nothing more, nothing less. Still, what "actually" happened is left for us to decide. From there, we invent stories about why it happened, preparing us for if it happens again.

We tell stories for everything: our identity, our personality, our history, our future. For others: why she acted that way, why he treated me this way. Because the mind believes in a coherent world, it is desperate to explain everything. So our thoughts attempt to explain the *why* of life, the how, the when, the where—all through story. Then we defend these mental constructs with more story.

The Indelible Ink of Story

The lingering effect of what happens in your life experience comes down to how it makes you *feel*. We remember the sensation of an event, and fill in the blanks with story.

We attach to thoughts and the way they make us feel. Story represents the culmination of our attachments in this lifetime. We use story to reason the ways of the world, who we are, who others are. We hold on tightly to our stories because they're familiar, they're safe.

Yet after you remove the ink from the pages of our story, what remains is Feeling. Add the ink back and you have your thoughts about those Feelings.

Feeling is always present. So by tapping in to Feeling, we return to presence. The more we can be present with our Feelings, the easier it is to be present in our entire experience.

Feelings are our guide into the present moment. Truly *feeling* anything requires the body to be fully alert and the mind to be fully aware. Only when we're present do we touch the moment with complete sensory awareness. The more present we are, the more richly we embrace unadulterated sensation—before attaching it to a story.

The Story's Mood

Just like your favorite novel takes on an overall tone, our stories carry these Feelings as an energy, a color, a texture, a sound—a *mood*. Mood is a story's Feeling. It is the back cover on a book telling you what to expect from the tale. It's romantic or suspenseful. It's exciting or terrifying. It's hopeful or depressing.

In either case, just a word. Just a thought.

A word, along with its interpretation, carries an emotional charge, a vibrational impact that resonates louder and louder, stronger and stronger the more we use it. The more we use it, the more we cement the association to the origin Feeling.

Mood is a state of mind. It's a mental concept. It's the mind perceiving sensation and labeling the energetic vibration. Mood, therefore, echoes throughout our experience. It compiles a soundtrack for our story and illustrates it with color.

Insight into our lives can be detected when looking at our mood. The words of our story create an energetic response, and so serve as persistent reminders of what the mind says we "should" be feeling whenever we hear, read or speak them. Basically, mood tells us what we're thinking and how that thought makes us feel.

Mood as a barometer for a cluttered mind is effective because of how closely mood is linked with our thinking (story). We know thoughts can litter the mind, but sometimes mood is the only access point for recognizing how deeply cluttered the mind might be, versus trying to monitor every thought.

We respond to the mood of a story with cultivated behavior. First, we feel. Next, we label the felt sensation and give it meaning. And finally, we act. Each phase a progressive energetic response.

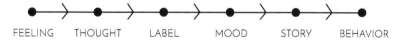

FEELING   THOUGHT   LABEL   MOOD   STORY   BEHAVIOR

Because we're constantly acting out our mood, when aware, we can see how negative behavior ties back to a negative mood. Or how positive behavior credits a positive mood. And so on.

Story and its accompanying mood determine our behavior in any moment. This is the reason why we might sabotage our chances at starting a business, because our story is, "I'll never make it," "I'll run out of money," or "I'm going to fall flat on my face and everyone will laugh." And so with that reluctant mood, we never even start. Meanwhile, at a standstill, we're always wondering, *what if.*

Or we might sabotage our marriage because our story is, "As long as he changes _____, and does _____ for me, we can get along." And so we wait until outside circumstances are different before we accept people back into our hearts. Meanwhile, our relationships suffer because we're holding out for others to change their behavior before we change ours.

Or we might sabotage our efforts to really declutter our lives because our story is that, "If only I could afford to build an addition to my house, I'd have more room to put away all my stuff and I'd feel much better about coming home." And so we don't take the time to look at our stuff, reevaluate if it "belongs" with us anymore and let go of what doesn't. Meanwhile, stuff stacks up in the garage and the house stays too small for everything we keep buying and we never tap in to *why.*

A Play On Words

Think of the words *can't, won't, shouldn't* and *don't.* How do they make you feel?

Think of the words *can, will, should* and *do.* How do they make you feel?

Notice a difference? I bet you did.

So, would it follow that, in life, if we change the words we use, we would get a different Feeling, a different mood?

Let's test it out. Sit comfortably in a chair, in a quiet place, with no distractions. Turn off the lights, or close the blinds. Now, use your senses to fully observe what a word does to your physical body.

Think of the word *summer.* Sit with it and your definition of what the word means. Embody the word. How does it make you feel? How does your body respond to this word? Take note of your face and the posture of your body the moment the word comes into focus.

Think of the word *gloom*. Sit with it and your definition of what the word means. Embody the word. How does it make you feel? How does your body respond to this word? Take note of your face and the posture of your body the moment the word comes into focus.

Think of the word *clean*. Sit with it and your definition of what the word means. Embody the word. How does it make you feel? How does your body respond to this word? Take note of your face and the posture of your body the moment the word comes into focus.

Think of the word *laughter*. Sit with it and your definition of what the word means. Embody the word. How does it make you feel? How does your body respond to this word? Take note of your face and the posture of your body the moment the word comes into focus.

Now open your eyes. Did you gain some insight on your reaction to certain words?

Funny how something as trivial as a *word* becomes what dictates our every move.

This exercise begins the lesson on mind-body awareness. True decluttering requires the awareness of mind and body. It involves *minding our minds* and monitoring our moods. Depending on where our mind is in any moment and how it affects our mood, our behavior responds accordingly. Our expression in the world (stance, disposition, countenance, action) responds accordingly.

We can think happy, encouraging thoughts and our bodies flutter off into the sunshine, skipping along after our minds. We can think negative, discouraging thoughts and our bodies hunch over in despair, wallowing in the crypts of our minds.

Since we always have *choice* (free will) on our side, it is possible for us to choose a better thought that would serve to foster a more empowered belief system, a happier mood and healthier behavior...which makes for an improved life experience. To do this—to choose this "better" thought—we merely have to be aware of our ability to do so. We merely have to know we *can*. ("And knowing is half the battle." -G.I. Joe)

Because mood is contingent on thought (mood *is* a thought), we can change our moods as easily as we change our thoughts. We can place ourselves in a happy state of mind after someone cuts us off on the freeway, choosing to believe that the "driver must be late to work so I'll get out of her way and not slow her down."

If we change our minds at the level of perception (cleaning up our thoughts), we can effect a different mood and therefore a different behavior instantaneously. Choosing a better thought is like deliberately sweeping away dirt; we're slowly dusting off filthy words in favor of words that foster clarity and well-being.

We can monitor our mood as a way inward—into our thoughts—where we begin our cleaning.

CHAPTER 6

THE MIND

The mind is amazing. It sparks ideas that build both businesses and nations. It crafts amazing stories, paintings and buildings. From the interlacing scaffolding of our minds, we construct the edifice of our lives, with thought as the building blocks.

Nothing exists for you outside of your ability to experience it within the framework of your mind. We can't see beyond the limits set by our mind.

What your mind believes represents Truth as you know it. And everything either contradicts or confirms this Truth. Your life, this universe, heaven, hell, are each subject to your beliefs about it (and to the *stories* you tell).

Life is just a mind-made story. It begins and ends in our minds.

The mind uses the body as the means with which to explore and navigate life. The more connected mind and body are in the exploration, the greater the insight. As open and aware the mind is, is as daring and curious as the body will be.

Our limited purview, while it may seem vast, is but a tiny pixel in the big picture. The more cluttered our mind, the more limited our view. The more limited our steps. The more limited our freedom. Clutter stifles and suffocates our divine right to live free, peaceful and clear.

It is important to understand the mind more fully so we can easily recognize a clear mind from cluttered mind. You'll come to discover, as I did several years ago, that the cause of and cure for clutter are one and the same.

Let's explore that idea with a story.

The Mind as a Tool

The world is our laboratory where we get to experiment with decision, activity, experiences, growth and change. We enter this laboratory upon our birth as *scientists*, full of curiosity. In this experiment we call life, we're met with endless choices, ideas, concepts and other world phenomena to test and discover.

In the lab, the mind is our go-to tool for all of our experiments. This tool has features galore like a Swiss Army survival kit, the chief one being a compass. It helps us explore and navigate the world, our test site. In the end, this tool makes a science (makes sense) of the experiential and environmental information it receives, and derives concepts, theories and assumptions in response. We study, observe, experiment and eventually intellectualize our findings. These become the rules of the lab.

We use the tool to lead us to safety, food and shelter. We use it to point the way and monitor our path—remembering, recording, offering suggestions, feedback and direction. To gauge the change in seasons—spring, summer, fall, winter—and prompt the body to slow down in the winter and speed up in the summer. To use the sunrise to wake the body and sunset to put it to sleep.

The needle of this tool's compass points us in all different directions during our experiments. Apart from pointing the way across the terrain of the world, setting our biological clock and guiding our way through relationships, career decisions, food choices, etc., we also gain access to a doorway beyond this world with the compass—to a place beyond body, time and form. A place we'll call consciousness (spirit). This doorway opens when we center the compass's needle toward true north. Once through that doorway, we experience more than what we could ever cognitively grasp with just our logical mind. Here, the mind connects us to consciousness—a direct line to God—like a treasure map connects pirates to gold.

When we hold steady north, the mind opens a portal into the vastness of consciousness. Consciousness is the vibrant part of us that takes responsibility for our journey, sees beauty in all things, finds opportunity everywhere, fears nothing and loves unconditionally. It is here that our mind is centered and calm.

Consciousness finds its focus on *formlessness* (intangibles; Feelings), without a need to operate in this world. It needs nothing from anything because it is everything. It is divinity, that universal energy that sees, knows, connects and unites us all. It thrives on *being*. Being goodness, inspiration, love.

When the compass's needle points anywhere but north, we're catapulted into a place called unconsciousness—that fragile part of us operating in this world of material concern, focused on survival of the body, keeping us alive, fed and rested. Unconsciousness moves through life as a victim or victor; reacts to life as painful or pleasurable; and looks at everything as something to do or avoid. It processes information, interprets experiences and borrows beliefs. It is the source of blame, complaints and judgment.

Unconsciousness finds its focus in *form* (tangibles; matter) in order to operate in the world. It needs form to feel steady and secure as it moves against the boundaries of finite objects it perceives in the world. Its tunnel-vision keeps it from omniscience and connection, restricting its level of awareness. It thrives on *doing*. Doing more, better, faster.

Our compass when centered in the north activates the spirit-mind, which is a decluttered, aware, intuitive state of mind. In any other direction, when the needle swings south, west or east, the compass is activating the body-mind, which is a survivalist, action-oriented state of mind.

Because of the surface level of its dealings, body-mind keeps our body alive and growing. Its number one concern is *progressing*. Actually, unconsciousness mistakes enlightenment for progress. It seeks progress in this lifetime—advancement of intellect, influence, and involvement—as a sign of self-actualization. It forgets the "self" it is ultimately serving, so it seeks earthly validation to stay on course. A course that's guided by survival and engrained in the rewards of this world.

Spirit-mind remembers the "self" it is serving, the *True Self*, the *you* deep inside. The you that is conscious. And spirit-mind knows enlightenment is a decluttered life experience. Freedom. Ease. It doesn't chase progress, accolades or credentials. Its merits are found in peace, love and joy.

Knowing the different directions we could go, as owner and operator, sometimes we need to put the tool down, step back and determine where the compass is leading us.

Calibrating the Tool

Like any good scientist, you detect that the compass on your tool (the mind) can point you in two opposing directions. So you might hypothesize that the mind is often torn between two diverging roles; one being its role as body-mind (action), and the other being its role as spirit-mind (awareness).

The spirit-mind is the observer-mind; it does the observing because it's tapped in to the conscious, omniscient you. The true you sits at the helm, behind your body, behind your mind, behind your thoughts, witnessing and acknowledging.

The body-mind is the survivalist-mind; it steers and supports the body. It sits on the front line, defending, protecting and going after base needs and desires.

SPIRIT-MIND	BODY-MIND
GPS	Driver
Observer-mind	Survivalist-mind
Intuition	Intelligence
Focused on formlessness	Focused on form
Driven by freedom	Driven by progress
Being	Doing
Consciousness	Unconsciousness
Awareness	Action
Centered	Scattered
Decluttered	Cluttered

If we imagined the body to be a car, body-mind would be the driver, and spirit-mind would be the GPS system with access to the map of the world. The driver can choose to listen to the turn-by-turn directions or not. If it doesn't listen, the car will eventually veer off the path, get lost, run out of gas, you name it. But the GPS is always recalibrating based on the car's current location, ready to offer up new, clear navigation.

Imagine if we always listened to the GPS?

Since we have this amazing tool at the ready, imagine if we let it serve us? We would want to take care of it and keep it in tip-top shape, of course. We would want to calibrate it often.

To calibrate the mind is to center its compass needle north and adjust our steps in order to bring balance. Whenever we do this, we usher in calm and clarity to our lives. From the standpoint of clarity, we allow the whole-mind (body-mind and spirit-mind) to do its thing without getting attached to either of its roles. To calibrate the tool, or balance the mind, is to detach.

I read a story in *The One Thing: The Surprisingly Simple Truth Behind Extraordinary Results* by Gary Keller that put everything in perspective for me when considering the roles of the body-mind and spirit-mind.

> *One evening an elder told his grandson about a battle that goes on inside all people. He said, "My son, the battle is between two wolves inside us. One is fear. It carries anxiety, concern, uncertainty, hesitancy, indecision and inaction. The other is Faith. It brings calm, conviction, confidence, enthusiasm, decisiveness, excitement and action." The grandson thought about it for a moment and then meekly asked his grandfather: "Which wolf wins?" The old Cherokee replied, "The one you feed."*

At any point, we're "feeding" a different part of our mind. Where our attention is at any time determines which part of the mind is getting nourished. When we focus on vengeance, the body-mind is fed. When we focus on compassion, the spirit-mind is fed.

And what we feed grows.

What part of the mind are you feeding in meditation? When playing sports? When reading a book? When sitting in a business seminar? Only you can answer those questions because you know where your attention is during those activities. We go into everything with an intention, which readies our attention, whether we discern it or not. What is your intention before you meditate? Before you play that game? Before you open that book? Before you walk into that seminar?

When it comes to the mind, we can feed the part that serves our connection to the divine, and subsequently moves us toward enlightenment and freedom. But that doesn't mean we must starve the other part. When balanced, we feed both parts adequately. A balanced "feeding schedule"—where neither is deprived—keeps us clear-headed and conscious while living our human life in this body.

Balance brings clarity to both roles. It centers a "scattered brain." Whatever we feed the mind is also feeding its habits and inclinations. We can feed our fears, or we can feed our trust in God.

It's also important which part of the mind we feed *first*. Think of how flight attendants instruct us to put the oxygen mask on ourselves before assisting others with theirs. When we replenish the spirit-mind first, it remains seated as the observer and doesn't get blinded by the fickle needs and desires of the body-mind. Instead, these needs and desires of the body-mind come into fresh perspective, viewed by the spirit-mind. This way, it's a lot easier to see if we're feeding a lie (fear, limiting belief, etc.) or feeding the Truth (love, abundance, etc.).

When we calibrate our tool, we bring all functions into balance—returning it to factory settings. We balance the two minds. The whole-mind then moves the body upon the earth while still remembering who we are underneath the skin and bones.

The mind serves us in various ways, like any state-of-the-art tool would. When we don't keep the mind tuned and calibrated, clutter begins to take shape. Our imbalance becomes our clutter.

CHAPTER 7

THE ROOT OF CLUTTER

Thoughts become things. Speculation turns to fact. Imagination turns to dogma. Illusion to reality.

The minute we form a thought in our minds, we turn visceral sensation (free-flowing energy) into an object (stuck energy). Thought breathes life into this "sense object," turning it into *matter*. These thoughts take shape (thoughtform) and take up space in our minds, where we make people, places and things *matter*. Nothing really matters except what we make matter, what we make important. Whatever matters to us only matters because we give it meaning, we give it a place in our lives.

We give it a name, a label, a definition. We think this label, speak this label, we attach a meaning, good or bad, to this label. Sadness, anger, grief. Delight, excitement, joy. Thought, thought, thought.

Clutter, by its very nature, distracts us from its dirty little secret: that it's only ever a manifestation of our thoughts.

At the root of all clutter *is* thought.

Clutter is clutter whether we cling to it or not. Regardless of what we do with it, clutter comes to adorn or disfigure, enhance or destroy. It pops up to tell us what we're supposed to be, supposed to do. It thinks we need "more" and "better" and "stronger" to fulfill our life purpose.

Add a "label" to one simple thought that subsequently triggers a reaction in us and watch how our energy quickly spirals toward destruction. Why do we let clutter fool us?

Clutter is charged with an energy of fear and lack because it exists solely to substitute, substantiate and symbolize. It trades Truth for lies. It swaps wholeness for weakness. We replace clarity with clutter in an attempt to fill our lives with mind-made meaning.

When we attach meaning to things, we are really just attaching to thoughts *about* those things. For instance, when we speak our first words, we attach to the idea of language. When we own a car, we attach to the idea of prestige whenever we drive it. When we marry, we attach to the idea that we'll be together until death. When others put a marker on our gravesite, they attach to the idea that our identity will live forever.

This attachment to thought, or mental concepts, gives the thought a longer life. Makes it endure as beliefs and stories. Makes it clutter.

When we cling to a thought or concept, for whatever solace it brings, it blurs the clarity of our minds. Spirit-mind gets upstaged by body-mind.

Mind Before Matter

Because thoughts are the root of clutter, clutter exists in our minds first and foremost. Nothing manifests externally unless first created internally. It's not just mind *over* matter, but more accurately, mind *before* matter.

What we see is a result of what we put there! **We're only ever projecting our mental mess into our world.** If we experience clutter in our environment, it means we first perceived in our minds debilitating thoughts about ourselves, our capabilities, our world…

What's going on in our heads shows up in our homes.

The Talmud says, "We see the world not as it is, but as we are." We project onto the world our expectations, our fears, our desires, our hopes. We project our perception of things. It becomes our prophecy and eventually our testimony as the mind looks for evidence to confirm its beliefs—and what we look for, we find. In this way, we create our own reality.

What we see is only a projection of our inside *stuff*, our mental clutter. Our sabotaging beliefs, our pain, our fear. And what everyone else sees is a projection of their inside stuff.

Yet we think everything is happening *to* us. This victim mindset is why we usually start out on a mission to clean out our closets, or dresser drawers, because our finger points outward (away from us). Cleaning on the surface level is not going to produce the penetrating results we seek because we're not cleaning deep enough.

What shows up in our environment as clutter is merely a projection of our internal state at the time. Some of the clutter in your life is a residual effect of a mental state you were in years ago, a cycle you're still on because the clutter is still around. But where you're at in your clutter cycle primarily reflects your current mental state.

Anything outside of you cannot affect you unless you let it. Even clutter affects us only to the extent that we *think* about it. The energy of thought keeps us preoccupied with clutter and therefore keeps it around.

How clutter comes to exist, is also how it continues to survive. How it is born is how it will die.

The cause of clutter is also the cure.

What we think.

Your behavior and environment are mere echoes of your thoughts. You hold the key to whether you hoard or don't hoard, love or don't love, hate or don't hate, enjoy or don't enjoy, just by the nature of your thinking and its contagious energy.

Can you maintain thoughts of clarity and awareness no *matter* what happens?

CHAPTER 8

THE COST OF CLUTTER

We've dispelled the ultimate myth, that clutter is all environmental. The big reveal: clutter is primarily mental.

Clutter is born, and endures, in the mind.

Clutter, mental or environmental, isn't *good* or *bad*. It just *is*. What we do with clutter and how we let it affect us inside and out, now that's where it gets sticky.

Whatever pollutes our minds inevitably shows up polluting our living space, our work space and our social space. A cluttered mind begets a cluttered body, heart, bank account and lifestyle. Two cluttered minds together beget cluttered relationships. A cluttered relationship begets a cluttered household. A cluttered household begets cluttered offspring. And on and on.

Clutter is contagious and seeps into everything.

What is clutter costing you? How is it keeping you from living a full life? Not only is it debilitating, stifling and exhausting, clutter causes discord, disorder and disconnection. It leads to overwhelm, thinking we have to know it all. It leads to overload, thinking we have to do it all. And it leads to overspeaking, thinking we have to say it all.

We're thinking too much.

We're thinking too much and cluttering our world.

If your environment is cluttered, you're already cluttered mentally, just like a thirsty person is already dehydrated. Overwhelm, overload and overspeaking are mental clutter. Each means we are stuck in over-thinking (clinging). We've attached to thoughts, concepts, beliefs long enough that now we're stuck in stress, fear and *dis-ease*.

We automatically curb clutter by becoming aware of it. Awareness is cleansing. Awareness and presence begin to clear clutter away. We can only take care of a mind and body we're aware of.

Awareness shines a flashlight onto the symptoms of clutter—when we recognize the effect, we can attend to the cause. Cluttered minds cause cluttered lives. Mental clutter most certainly becomes physical clutter.

We can see it in our environment. How is clutter pervading your life?

Look at your bedroom and compare the state of that area with the way you feel about your love life. What is the level of intimate vulner-ability in your relationship?

Look at your desk and compare the state of that area with the way you feel about your career. Are you happy with how far you're progress-ing professionally?

Look at your kitchen and compare the state of that area with the way you feel about your health. When was the last time you prepared a balanced meal at home instead of grabbing fast food?

Look at your closets and compare the state of that area with how you feel in your clothes. Do you own clothes that you haven't worn in over 12 months because they don't fit?

Look at your living room and compare the state of that area with your quality time with friends and family. Are you able to entertain company without apologizing for a messy home?

When we pay attention, we start to see the consequences of a clut-tered mind show up in our lives. Our environmental lives are the vis-ible effects of our mental lives.

Clutter Clues: The Symptoms of Mental Clutter

The visual effects of clutter are obvious. But the junk drawers, past-due bills, clothes piled on the floor indicate something deeper is going on. The non-visual effects of clutter show up as being scatter-brained, depressed or bored, for example.

There are eight effects, or symptoms, of clutter that I want to focus on in this book. These non-visual symptoms are confusion, chatter, chaos, conditions, collections, comparisons, commitments and control. (Don't get hung up on these labels. Instead, use them as your clutter clues.)

Let's go into each symptom.

CONFUSION

Confusion is a lack of clarity and understanding; uncertainty. It's being unclear about something. It feels like being scatterbrained and out of sorts. It is the onslaught of worry and fear; panic attacks.

It is when we are overanalyzing and our vision is muddled, foggy, cloudy, or unsettling. It's being unable to wrap your head around a given idea. It is endless processing and competing thoughts. Confusion results when the mind won't shut off even if the input is beyond what we can handle at that time.

It is when the body-mind is concerned with "figuring stuff out." When we take in information and try to make sense of it from a limited perspective.

The body-mind forgets that we need not overthink. We don't have to comprehend everything all at once or at the time of *sensing*—we can simply acknowledge and allow our innate wisdom the time to clarify.

Confusion as a symptom of clutter reminds us that we don't have to know it all! Confusion begets overwhelm. It is a sign that our minds are flustered with trying to process a new concept, and it might be time to put some distance between you and the thought. Allow spirit-mind the space to reveal clarity around the topic.

CHATTER

Chatter is the ongoing narrative in the back of our heads. It's noise. It's the jibbering, jabbering and everyday inner dialogue. Chatter feels like incessant mental dialogue, droning on in the background, curious, impatient, explaining.

It is when that small voice inside rants about love and loss, about successes and failures, about why and why not. It could be recounting the happiest moments in life or bemoaning the saddest day in history. Chatter sounds like anything that disrupts and disturbs the quiet.

It is when the body-mind is concerned with filling the space and avoiding "awkward" silence. Silence is only awkward if we think it is; otherwise, it's a welcomed blessing in a noisy world.

The body-mind forgets that we need not overspeak. We don't have to say everything that comes to mind. We don't have to let our inner chatterbox consume us.

Chatter as a symptom of clutter reminds us that we need a break from the chitchat going on between our ears. It shows us that we can benefit from taking some quiet time. By calming the chatter inside, we will experience a less noisy outside.

CHAOS

Chaos is the complete disorder, disarray, disorganization and disruption in our heads. Chaos amounts to mental anarchy. It feels like having no order or organization amidst dissenting ideas and beliefs.

It is a mutiny of thought; the disturbance of peace. The overthrow of composure by demands, activity and incessant doing.

It is when the body-mind is overcome by jumbled desires and destinations. When it is concerned with having it all, being it all, doing it all. Chaos is when we believe that we have to be all things to all people, the jack of all trades, and we have to impress the masses.

The body-mind forgets that we need not overwhelm ourselves. We don't have to take on more than we can handle, or get derailed from our real priorities.

Chaos as a symptom of clutter reminds us that we are caught in the eye of the storm. Too much is happening at once, all vying for our attention. And we inundate ourselves with too many *should*s and *must*s, like bees buzzing around our heads. Calm the storm by saying no when it feels like no. What do *you* really want to do? Do that.

CONDITIONS

A condition is defined as a stipulation, prerequisite or requirement. Conditions are also the factors influencing the progression or outcome of a situation. They are the demands and expectations we place on ourselves and others. Conditions feel like rules, boundaries and limits.

It is when we require things from people or objects so that we feel better about ourselves. When we place conditions on our relationships, we're choosing predictability over acceptance. Conditions in relationships are when we require certain behavior from others so we're comfortable in our own skin. Conditions in business are when we demand that others meet certain performance criteria to bring about our desired result.

It is when the body-mind acts as survivalist, setting conditions as a way of preventing our discomfort or death.

The body-mind forgets that we need not overanalyze. By overanalyzing, we're preparing for the worst. We're gearing up for battle while padding the edges of life with bubble-wrap hoping not to get hurt.

Conditions as a symptom of clutter remind us that we're going against the flow by placing expectations on the pace and order of life. That we're not accepting life as it comes, and instead resisting its perfect unfolding. When we allow life to unfold as it will, we allow ourselves to see and receive the goodness that awaits.

COLLECTIONS

Collections are the gathering and grouping of objects (and anything we make an object, including people). They are the stockpiling of prestige, security and comfort. Collections feel like trophies, acknowledgment and validation.

It is when we collect thoughts. Memories, beliefs, stories, traditions. We hoard reasons, rationales, theories and moments.

It is when the body-mind gathers thoughts that make us feel comfortable. We hang onto them for a time (or forever) because we've become attached to their story. We like the thought of keeping it around to always bring us that feeling.

The body-mind forgets that we need not overload ourselves. We overload ourselves with stuff because we rely on it for the feeling it first brought us. But we don't have to *have* everything. We are full and complete just as we are. We lack nothing because we are *one* with everything.

Collections as a symptom of clutter remind us that we are attaching to thoughts about the past, present or future. That we are letting clutter take up space in our heads instead of freeing ourselves of its bondage and living without its weight.

COMPARISONS

Comparisons are the formation of comparative or superlative judgments. It is deliberately taking two things and pitting them against each other for the sake of choosing a preference, or winner. It feels like judging two options to decide which is preferred. It feels like searching for *bigger* and *better*, or like chasing *faster* and *stronger*.

It is when we are preoccupied with *what if*. When we compete with our former selves, our current selves and our future selves. Then we rate that against the appearance and achievements of others. Always looking to exceed benchmarks, meet higher goals, and improve for tomorrow.

It is when the body-mind seeks validation as a sign of progress. We look to things outside of ourselves in order to boost confidence, and end up tearing it down. We compare people, places, objects, ideas, theories and lifestyles. We compare ex-husband to new husband. Old girlfriend to new girlfriend. Bad friends to good friends. And we form biases, judgments and prejudices based on what comes of these comparisons. Really, when comparing, we are only ever comparing one thought about something to another thought about the same thing—all in our minds.

The body-mind forgets that we need not overcompensate. We believe we are lacking something and so spend our days measuring up to this arbitrary idea of wholeness. How exhausting to compete with everything that comes our way rather than embracing what comes!

Comparisons as a symptom of clutter remind us that we're not accepting ourselves. That we're fighting against who we are as if we can exchange the package we came in. You are enough. You might just need a shift in mindset to see that. Might sound cheesy, but when we stop competing, we win.

COMMITMENTS

Commitments are when energy is allocated to different causes or activities within a certain timeframe. We commit with both attention (mind) and action (body) to all sorts of things: family, work, money, diet, dates, meetings, projects and more. Commitment feels like filling calendars with appointments. It feels like writing lists of to-dos.

It is when we give something our focus. When we give something our focus, we are saying yes to it. We want it. What we commit to is our decision; even mandates and obligations are ultimately subject to our willingness. When we give of ourselves to something or someone, we've willfully chosen not to give of ourselves elsewhere.

It is when the body-mind commits as if out of obligation or guilt. By committing, we're placing an expectation on our capability and capacity to do that thing. Cluttered is doing one thing while being preoccupied with what we're *not* doing.

The body-mind forgets that we need not overcommit. We don't have to say yes to everything to please others or meet a quota. We can make time to do nothing, and life will still go on.

Commitments as a symptom of clutter remind us that by placing unmanageable demands on our time we lose clarity. Committing can feel overwhelming when we put too much on our plate and spread ourselves too thin. When we believe we have to be everywhere, doing everything, we're bound to wear out. It means we haven't given ourselves room to *be*.

CONTROL

Control is the power to influence behavior or the course of events. Through control, we seek to commandeer the performance and behavior of life, of other people, in order to reap our preferred outcome. It feels like managing and manipulating circumstances so that we're more comfortable.

It is when our inner perfectionist creates contingencies, obligations, rubrics, protocols, procedures, guides, dogma—and protests when things don't go as planned. It is seeking unconditional love and happiness though control.

It is when the body-mind thinks we have to orchestrate people, places and things in order to be protected. We believe we can affect our internal state with the rearranging of the external world. Thinking what is outside has to change before we can change.

The body-mind forgets that we need not overplan. We don't have to tailor every aspect of life according to our agenda. There are things we have control over because they reside in us, like how we view the world, and there are things we don't. We can let what we don't control simply be, and get out of its way.

Control as a symptom of clutter reminds us that we are resisting instead of allowing. We can't begin to fathom what God will bestow upon us—a life greater than our wildest imagination. But only if we allow it. We have the free will to resist. Like a movie director, God knows the big picture. Let go and let God. And rather than attempt to bring the entire production under your control, focus on your role in the movie. Focus on your story.

The Effects of Mental Clutter

Mental clutter is debilitating, as we can imagine given its symptoms. It weakens our mental wherewithal, our mental stamina and our mental strength. When the mind is weak, the body becomes weak; it atrophies. It conforms to the limitations set by the mind. If the mind loses the conviction of its own worth and power, it won't believe it can do extraordinary, amazing things. It will set ceilings for how high it believes it can go. It won't tell the body to perform at a high level, but let it cave to an inferior, helpless path. And the body knows nothing but to submit to the mind; muscles, organs and joints all surrender to the mind.

Let's go through each of the eight symptoms of clutter and visualize cause and effect. Take two minutes per scenario to envision yourself in these situations. Really connect with how you would feel given the respective mindset.

CONFUSION

1. After months of couples therapy with your husband, you two still can't seem to get over the past. You won't forgive him about something he did, and he won't forgive you for making him do it. How hopeful are you about the future of your relationship?
2. There are papers everywhere on your desk, invoices, receipts, marketing flyers, notes, and you can't keep track of what day it is, let alone find anything you need when you need it. How confident do you feel about your ability to manage your personal and professional life?

CHATTER

1. All around you at work is noise and gossip. You eventually join the conversation, throwing your complaints and judgments around. How does talking negatively like this make you feel about yourself?
2. The news spews out horror story after horror story, yet you continue to tune in. Stats, deficits, verdicts and doctors' opinions begin to blur together. How safe do you feel leaving your house every day?

CHAOS

1. You wake up in the morning and immediately start rushing around, getting dressed, making breakfast, running to meet clients, grabbing take-out for dinner, and you hit your pillow exhausted that night. How eager are you to do it all over again the next day?
2. Toys are everywhere, stains cover the carpets, dirty dishes fill the sink and no one's cleaning up after themselves. It looks like you live with a bunch of wild animals. Not to mention there's no quiet space in the entire house to go to escape them. How friendly do you feel toward each member of the household?

CONDITIONS

1. The relationship with your children is strained. They blame you for everything you've ever done wrong raising them, and you feel like

you didn't do anything right. You've all become estranged without you fully understanding where you fell short as a parent. How lovable do you feel?

2. Every assistant you hire ends up getting fired. They blame lack of training, but you think it is lack of skill. You have expectations for how you want the work to be done but they keep falling short. How supported and supportive do you feel?

COLLECTIONS

1. Every 1st of January, you renew your gym membership, setting the resolution to lose 20 pounds by December 31st, and every year your gym membership goes unused. How do you feel about collecting years of wasted dues and unmet goals?

2. You proudly display your souvenirs, trophies and funny tchotchkes on your mantelpiece. When people come over, they go to admire them only to find them dusty and crowded, while you give backstories for every single one. How would you feel if your guests suggested you throw all that stuff away?

COMPARISONS

1. You're getting dressed for an evening out and you start comparing yourself to a model you saw in a magazine. You notice your hips are bigger than hers, you aren't as tall and your hair isn't as blonde. How sexy do you feel about going out in your clothes?

2. As you're moving through postures in yoga class, you glance over at a neighboring yogi and begin comparing your novice moves with her expert, ballerina-like moves. How strong and present do you feel moving in and out of Downward Facing Dog, balancing in Warrior 3, and holding Crescent Lunge?

COMMITMENTS

1. As you schedule business meeting after business meeting, you fill your calendar leaving no time to breathe. Meanwhile, you're not eating healthy meals, you barely sleep three hours a night, and you haven't seen your friends in months. How balanced do you feel?

2. As you take on more projects that don't excite you, clients that don't respect you, and hours that leave bags under your eyes, it looks like you've created a job for yourself instead of a business. Not only that but being the perfectionist you are, you're committed to doing everything right, which, to you, means doing everything yourself. How does your predicament make you feel about being an entrepreneur?

CONTROL

1. You start your day with an ambitious to-do list and you set out to get it all done. But by the end of the day, you have half of the tasks left unchecked. You add those things to tomorrow's to-do list as the overall list gets longer and longer. How do you feel about everything that stood in the way of accomplishing the day's objectives (namely yourself)?

2. You started dating a gorgeous man. He's sweet, charming, flirty and fun. This draws you to him, but also makes you jealous when you see him with other women. So you steal his passwords, check his text messages and email, and monitor his whereabouts, telling him where he can go and with whom. How does your lack of trust in him (and your new role as detective) cause you to talk about him to friends and family?

Hopefully you did the entire exercise above and didn't just skim through it. Give it another chance if you skipped ahead. Go back and sit with the feelings of each scenario, one by one. It's great practice for what's ahead.

Now that you finished, what do you think?

Did you find it easy to feel your way through these scenarios? Do you see how mental clutter skews and tweaks your perception of a situation? How likely it would be to fall in to victimhood, blame and envy? Or call it quits?

Well, I've got good news. Because you tuned into your Feelings in this exercise, and are tapping in to sensation more consistently, you are on your way to decluttering your life.

Feeling is the key.

CHAPTER 9

UNDERNEATH THE CLUTTER

Clearing mental clutter is like peeling an onion. Imagine we're trying to peel off every layer to get to the innermost bulb. That's what decluttering does for the mind; peels back every thought, every concept, every story. *And sometimes it makes us cry*. We peel away that which our cluttered thoughts made us believe (make-believe) to get down to our Truth.

Why live under a lie?

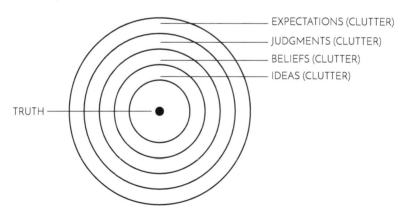

Who we truly are, without the fear, the lack, the overwhelm, is underneath the clutter. Maybe we won't get rid of clutter completely, but at least we can recognize it for what it is. Let's tear off the last layer of this onion to look even deeper.

There is a river of energy that flows, unencumbered and free, moving along a path with no obstacles. Its wide, continuous flow connects everyone to everything. Young and suggestible, we come to the river, drawn to the freedom it promises. We eagerly approach the water, hop onto our raft, untie the rope and pull out from the dock, into the current. And we ride along this river with our compass in hand. We're moving with the current, northbound. Things are great.

From this euphoria, we get an idea. We get curious and daring. We start to notice our surroundings. Maybe now we hear neighboring commuters boasting of all the things they've seen on their journey. We want to see them, too. We look and admire other faster, more expensive rafts. We want faster, too. Now we're getting scared, fearful of how we measure up, how fast we're going, and where the river ends. Slowly, we begin to veer off course. We move east, west, then south, against the current. Out of pure volition, we float astray, fighting the current, moving in the opposite direction of its flow.

Soon we get banked in the side brush, stuck in mud. Now we're completely turned around, lost.

Along the way, we forgot that if we just turn our raft back in the direction of the current, our ride will return to smooth and enjoyable. No more resisting the current, but rather going with its flow.

Life is the raft in this analogy. And the river is universal energy. As we face challenges, we forget this energy is always in perfect flow. So often we're paddling against the flow, wondering the cause of our struggle.

When we attach to mental concepts, we resist the flow. We turn the flow of energy into something that doesn't move and stays stagnant. We stand as roadblocks in the face of flow, fighting the current.

Energy wants to move freely, but when we cling to story and set restrictions, we trap and stifle its normal flow in, out and through. All because we expect (demand) something different. We expect everything to always perform like typecast characters in our story.

The minute we hijack energy's free flow is the minute we start to feel lethargic, sabotaged and stuck. The minute energy is suffocated,

our clothes don't get picked up, our relationships suffer from posses-
siveness and jealousy, and our kitchens get stocked with processed,
sugary foods.

Clutter spreads.

Our energy within affects energy without. What happens inside
happens outside. If I'm not letting energy flow freely through and
around me, then I'm going to witness energy stop flowing freely in my
surroundings, in my relationships and in my home. The clutter cycle
goes from thought to behavior to environment, and back around again.

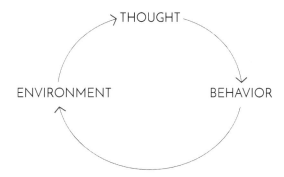

To declutter our lives, we have to let this energy free, let it move
in and out of everything without trying to store it and keep it forever.
Clinging only clutters our lives.

Clinging is when we're fearful on our raft, holding on for dear life,
resisting, fighting. We forget that we are safe if we just let go and go
with the flow.

Flow is freedom from struggle. Flow is consciousness.

Consciousness and Unconsciousness

Consciousness, or spirit-mind, keeps our raft afloat, buoyantly accepting
whatever rockiness or turbulence the river brings. It is "going with the
flow." Unconsciousness, or body-mind, reacts to every ripple and every
pebble, actively steering against the obstructions and believing it has to
brace itself for the next interference. We get so worked up in this effort
that we start to hate the journey. Struggling against the current makes
the ride worse. This is our unconscious resistance; we're resisting the flow.

Consciousness reminds us to slow down and see what we're doing to ourselves, how we're our own obstacle to flow and peace, how our reactions create hurdles, limitations and chaos.

The conscious mind is where we get clarity, courage and compassion. This part of the mind is the plug that connects us to the electrical outlet of Source—our power supply. Once we are plugged into Source, the energy surge channels peace, knowledge and contentment—because the Source *is* peace, knowledge and contentment. It is God, pure consciousness, spirit…you pick the label.

This Source energy is shared by all and therefore unites us all; it is our spiritual bloodline. This energy seeks expression through every living thing. We can tap in to that spiritual power whenever we remember that we always have access.

When we aren't plugged into Source, we are dwelling in unconsciousness. The longer we stay there, the higher the clutter mounts up and hides who we are underneath.

When we dwell in consciousness, we're free from concepts; decluttered. Free as birds, floating to the rhythm of life as it comes, with no pressures, stressors or demands.

The minute we think about life in terms of pressure, stress or demands, we start to place expectations, limitations and requirements on our existence. And our raft drifts off course.

Because of its connection to Source, consciousness keeps our minds free from disparaging thoughts and limiting beliefs. It's when unconsciousness battles for center stage that we lose sight of our inherent power and we loosen our grip on peace.

CHAPTER 10

WHY WE HOARD

Why do we hoard? Isn't that the question of a lifetime.

If the cost of clutter is so high as to be detrimental to our well-being, why do we do it?

Why do we hang on to beliefs and habits that sabotage our relationships, our productivity and our quality of life?

Why do we go shopping to deal with stress? Why do we drink or do drugs to escape our lives?

Because we're scared. Our body-mind is scared of the unknown. So we hoard what comforts us and provides some level of familiarity and safety.

Fearful thoughts like this are what prompt us to struggle on our raft. We think we have to hold on to unforgiveness to remind us why we hate someone so we don't get hurt again. Or that we should give up our efforts to start a project so we can avoid the humiliation of failure.

When we're scared, we hoard fearful energy.

The Search for Security

We are constantly searching for safety. Safety in the form of attention, appreciation and validation. So as we run after this idea of safety, our raft veers off course and we start collecting lovers, friends, possessions and degrees.

This search of ours is fueled by an energy of fear. And it has us hunting down pieces of brick to build a wall of protection around us.

This wall becomes one's identity.

In catering to our fear and carrying this wall, we make every step heavy and burdened. We are now preoccupied with protecting the *wall*. We have to keep all the pieces cemented in place because if one gets loose, the entire wall will come crumbling down. So the fear that built the wall in the first place never left but instead grew stronger.

What we feed grows.

As we construct an identity, we essentially bury our True Selves underneath. We bury our innate power underneath stories about who we are because we believe they make us safer, stronger and more lovable. We hide behind a name and a personality.

Our hoarding traits and characteristics to create an identity blind us to the truth of who we are. We begin to define ourselves by these mental concepts, rather than by the purity of spirit—who we are before and without human form.

We hoard because along the river, we became insecure, doubtful that we are and have enough. So we started to build this person the world would accept. We started to believe that by giving the world someone it wants, the world would always respond favorably and we wouldn't be vulnerable to the unknown. We started to build this character of ours on false pretenses.

Insecurity leads us to overthink, overcompensate, overspeak and overanalyze because we are desperate to feel secure in our own skin. The moment we first felt insecure as a young child, felt that we weren't safe, is the moment we began to bond to our first belief, to our first memory, to hold tight our first blankey, our first word.

Insecurity leads us to cling, hoard and bind ourselves to whatever we associate with the feeling of safety. We collect tokens of security in the form of clutter to buy us what we feel is lacking. Yet everything we need came to us at birth.

True security is peace. It is love and awareness. To remember that we cannot be harmed by the world is to return to peace, love and awareness. There is nothing to fear. We are safe.

We don't have to hide behind a wall.

When we stop clinging, we're free to love fully, embrace fully and fully let go. Let go of the searching and discover that what we were searching for was there all along.

Freedom from Clutter

If mental clutter feels like stifled, fearful and resistant energy, what does it feel like to be *free* from clutter?

It feels like clarity. Clarity is mental clutter cleared; a clear state of mind. It is the ability to see through clutter down to our core. At our core, we possess nothing, yet we are everything. We see ourselves whole and safe, just as we are.

Clarity is awareness, a balanced connection with both spirit-mind and body-mind. It is discernment and intuition. It is a gift from God.

Clarity is freedom from anxiety and overwhelm. It is freedom from overthinking, overload and overcompensation because when we are clear-headed we don't chase what is "lacking."

Clarity is freedom from form. From attachments.

We can always gauge our level of clarity by the quality of peace we feel (helpful hint: tap in to your mood). Peace, after all, isn't something we manufacture, collect or control. **Peace we** *feel*.

A clear mind is a peaceful mind.

Fear bulldozes a peaceful mind. Clarity will always get soiled by the need to feel safe. We form beliefs, customs, traditions and laws all in this effort, and we end up muddying the waters.

With restored clarity comes the ability to conceive, and perceive, our divine protection and provision. Then there's no reason to hoard, no reason to hold on to anything.

The clarity we had at birth comes again for most people on their deathbed. When it's very obvious that you can't take anything with you, you let it all go. Identity included. It takes dying for some to see the light.

Our thoughts, our beliefs and our perspective on the world represent our mental health. How can we begin to take care of our minds and restore clarity and peace so that there's no reason to cling to fear? How can we begin to declutter?

We can start by clearing our heads so we can create the space to discern truth from non-truth, consciousness from unconsciousness, flow from resistance.

CHAPTER 11

USING CLUTTER TO CLEAR CLUTTER

Beauty is in the eye of the beholder because what we see on the outside is evidence of what's going on inside of us. If we find nature's serene stillness beautiful, it means we appreciate that same nature in ourselves. We see what we are. The calmer we are inside, the easier it is to notice the indescribable beauty of a sunny morning or a starlit sky.

Seeing nature, people, places, things as beautiful requires that we clear out the ugly junk standing in the way. This junk is corroding our lenses. Our lenses need to be cleaned not from the outside, but from the inside. But not everyone knows to start from that side.

My decluttering journey certainly didn't start on the inside.

I remember it like it was yesterday. It was 2006 and I walked into my first yoga class with my mat and water bottle in hand, and the goal of getting flexible. I thought if I wasn't "bendy" now, I had to get bendy ASAP to prevent even tighter muscles as I aged. I had aspirations to be a flexible 80-year-old. And I heard yoga was a great place to start.

Well, that first class changed my perception of yoga. It wasn't just about flexibility. During class, I experienced a mind-body connection like never before. I saw how my mind instructed my body to move. I saw how in sync I was with my neighbor. I felt myself energetically bonding with the strangers around me as if we were battling the same fears and anxieties, right before we surrendered them onto our mat.

I can hardly describe the feeling, but it was palpable. I humbly welcomed the gracious instruction that the teacher bestowed upon me and the 20 other practitioners on their mats that morning.

There was a distinct part of me listening to the teacher, following her cues to get into each posture, and then there was another part of me that hovered and stood watch. This part observed the entire session, floating above me as I moved, watching me without judgment, only compassion. I felt loved and inspired, and motivated to love and inspire. Motivated to love on my body for its strength and abilities. Giving it gratitude for holding me up each day.

I walked out of there on a high. Skipping along, bowing to everyone in sight. Namaste.

Yoga isn't just for stretching—although flexibility has been a great side-effect of my continued practice. It is for clarity of mind.

It was obvious to me that yoga, and my discipline therein, was gifting me with a clearer mind, greater attentiveness to my body and any areas of imbalance. Months in, my thoughts began to slow down and change. I upgraded my inner dialogue from "I'm not flexible" to "I'm growing in flexibility."

I've grown in compassion for myself, for my body, for others and for their bodies. I've grown in patience for everyone and everything, seeing the value of waiting before passing judgment…and then realizing none needs to be passed at all.

And this isn't just me being airy-fairy. I genuinely credit yoga for opening my mind's eye to my inner chatter so I could see (and hear) how it affected my whole-being.

When the student is ready, the teacher appears. I was the student, and when I was ready, everything held a lesson. I let everything be an opportunity for surrender and compassion. Before, I was lost in confusion and overwhelm. I hadn't slowed down to take inventory of what I knew. Yoga helped me usher in the knowing I already had. To listen from within. The teacher appeared and she was me.

My point in bringing up yoga is to show that there's a physical layer and a nonphysical layer to everything in this lifetime. We might have to start with the physical layer to get to the nonphysical layer (remember the onion analogy?), but as we dive deeper within, we gain the insight to see clearer without. Just like in yoga, we turn our attention toward the body and eventually we get to the mind.

Now that we know the root of clutter, we can use external clutter (home, office, relationships) to detect internal clutter just as we use internal clutter to detect external clutter. The cycle works both ways.

Sometimes we need guidance to see through the fog in our minds and move us out of the way of peace. Sometimes we need guidance from the outside (a teacher, coach, etc.) in order to tap in to our awareness and discover our internal mess. We might need to start cleaning our kitchen, for instance, to see the impact food has on our health.

This is why the Declutter Code was created. It is your guide to clear both mental and environmental clutter by focusing on the mind first—because once the mind is clear, everything else can be cleared.

With consistent practice of the Code, you won't need to see environmental clutter before you instinctively detect your mental clutter. And once the Code becomes part of your every day and your sensory perception heightens as a result, the less you'll even need the Code as a guide. You will have found your innate clarity—the goal of decluttering.

Until then, use any point of entry (thought, mood, or environment) to detect a cluttered mind. Whichever way you can tap in to clarity, that is where you begin. Then drill deeper from there with inner inquiry.

What does my thinking sound like?
What does my mood feel like?
What does my environment look like?

If you can't hear your thoughts, but only feel your mood or see your behavior, then use that area to guide you toward an awareness of clutter—to wherever it has piled up in your life. As long as you are present and aware, you will begin to see patterns and clues as to what you are clinging to. From that place, you can loosen the ties that bind. Whatever step you take to clear clutter is promising, as long as you take a step.

Eventually, the steps lead *in*.

PART 2

CLEARING CLUTTER

The day you stop racing is the day you win the race.
—BOB MARLEY

CHAPTER 12

CLEARING CLUTTER WE DON'T SEE

How do we clear the clutter we don't see? How do we declutter something so elusive and intangible as the junk in our minds?

Great question. I've been asking myself this for years and I've been studying and learning how to do so. My journey to discovery hasn't been easy or cheap.

I started out looking to organize my bedroom. Then my kitchen. Then my office. I've stumbled upon a few roadblocks and made a couple wrong turns. It has cost me time, money, energy and space. I read books, followed procedures, listened to advice, sat in on seminars, attended workshops, and didn't find anything that made a lasting impact on my cluttered life.

In trying to rid clutter, I was only adding more. I was collecting all the ways that didn't work. So, then, not only was I cluttered, but I was more confused than ever. As I chased these so-called remedies, I was straying further and further from the answer.

I knew there was another way. (Yoga helped me see that much.) So I became the guinea pig.

I took all the information I'd learned, combined it with my own instinct and firsthand experience and created a system to declutter my life—a system I still use to this day. (Take my advice, clutter and stressors come daily, so the least we can do is declutter daily. Think of it as a lifestyle, not a diet.)

That system is called the *Declutter Code* and I'm going to walk you through the steps in the next chapter.

First, let me introduce you.

The Declutter Code is a practical yet profound ten-step process designed to clear mental clutter by bringing it out into the light. Like darkness, clutter can't exist where there is light.

Unlike scientific or governmental codes, the Declutter Code isn't a rigid rubric with consequences or penalties. It is not intended to be a law, rule or regulation. It is no mandate. Instead, the Code offers easy-to-follow techniques to remind us how to return to peace. You can follow the steps or not; the choice is always yours.

Because the Code is so simple, you won't be disappointed with yourself because follow-through is possible each and every time you use it. So use it often. It won't overwhelm or add more stuff to your plate. Rather, in decluttering our lives, we're removing the futile efforts that distract us from effectiveness, and we focus on powerful action.

There is a delicate order in the Declutter Code, as noted by the numbers one through ten. There's purpose in the order and the activities within each step, each one building off the one before. Granted, this is by no means a hard, fast rule, because doing just one of the ten steps is tantamount to making huge strides toward clarity. Just doing one thing on the list will skyrocket you lightyears toward a decluttered life, as opposed to doing none of them. But I do recommend you follow all of the steps in order for the most impactful transformation.

Don't put pressure on yourself or the Code to "work" in a certain way—you'll only go in with demands and end up overwhelmed and frustrated. This process will take intentional discipline to see what it can do for you, yes. But this process is to be easy. If it doesn't feel that way at first, it will become that way the more often you implement it.

There's freedom in discipline.

The Declutter Code is our flashlight, our vacuum and our dustpan. It will shine light on our hoarding and help clear the way to peace, clarity and freedom. It accomplishes this by offering steps to calm the chaos and clear the fog in our minds. It encourages restoring full-body awareness and the use of our six senses.

Like I revealed at the beginning of the book, the key to decluttering the mind lies in the ability to decipher form (thought) from Feeling (sensation). Form is an illusion; a figment of our imagination. Feeling is Truth. The Code was created to help us make the distinction.

Imagine that the next few pages of this book could change your life. Imagine that it can transform you if only you allow it to work its magic.

Today we begin anew, with new awareness and new action.

The Mental Warm-Up

Now that we've gone over what clutter is and how it shows up, we're finally ready to clear it away. Before we begin, let's get into the proper state of mind.

Picture your mind like a house. In order to clean this house, you'll have to separate losers from keepers. What do you want to get rid of? What do you want to keep?

You'll have to scour floor to ceiling, taking inventory, clearing cobwebs. You have to sweep behind dressers and sofas, under rugs. Dust the lampshades and light fixtures. You have to hose the dirt off the front porch and steps.

And, most importantly, you have to open windows and doors to let the sunshine in and the air flow through.

This same attention to detail goes for cleaning the recesses of our minds. The way to clear mental clutter is to clean like we would any drawer, closet or room in our homes. We need to deliberately go in, clear out the unnecessary and make space for clarity. We need to clear some beliefs away before adding more empowering information back in, or we can leave that open space empty (I imagine the latter being what Buddha would suggest).

All in all, be open to the process. Let go of inhibition and be light about it. Be patient and compassionate with yourself through the process. Where you are now, cluttered or clear, is perfect. Let what has happened in your life thus far be what has happened in your life thus far. Neither good nor bad, right nor wrong.

And, just for a moment, pretend that you've been given a box with a lock on it, but you lost the key somewhere and can't find it. You've tried everything to open this thing. Car keys, house keys, you've even tried picking the lock, but nothing's worked. Then one day, you found it, in plain sight, lying on your kitchen counter. You immediately know it's a match. You run upstairs with the key in hand and you grab the box. You stick the key into the lock and it's a perfect fit. And now you begin to turn...

Together, let's unlock and open our minds. Let's use our flashlight (insight) to sort through the losers and the keepers in our mental household.

CHAPTER 13

THE DECLUTTER CODE

Presented in the next few pages is The Declutter Code, your ten-step journey to clarity.

For our purposes, I've given each of the ten steps a name, a description, an explanation and a game plan. Forgive me for the clutter, *wink wink*. I do it this way because I want to help you comprehend the steps intellectually and experientially. Use these suggestions to guide you to your Feeling place and hone mind-body awareness. They will help you Feel your way through and serve as a catalyst for creating your own steps to clarity. Once through the ten steps, you'll have more insight into yourself and your thought patterns in order to do so.

Attend To You

The Declutter Code relies on your attention and intention. An intention to set the tone and attention to keep you focused.

The intention I'd recommend you set is, "I am open to receive insight." Receive the information that resonates with you, discard the rest. Let your attention be on your mind and body during the experiments. Listen to the small voice inside. Monitor your thoughts, your mood, your behavior and your reactions.

Quiet, alone time is most conducive to preparing for the Declutter Code. It helps you process and perform most of the experiments for each step. I usually go for walks in nature, sit in my bedroom with the door closed, or even grab a chair at the library. The space helps me center my attention and remove distractions.

As you read through and experiment with the Code, give yourself this time. Be generous with yourself, and don't feel bad about it. This selfish act is the most *selfless* we can be. Be patient and compassionate with yourself so you can extend the same to the world.

Pace Yourself

Each step of the Declutter Code offers you a game plan so you can practice it out in the world. I call them *experiments* because we are just like scientists observing mind-body awareness in our lab. Each experiment will take you through seven days of practice at home, in the office and in your relationships.

So we'll spend one full week, seven full days (e.g. Monday through Sunday), on each step of the Declutter Code so you make space to spend time with the results of the experiments.

With ten steps to the Code, it will take you ten weeks to complete them all. If that sounds like a lifetime, take a deep breath. You're already getting ahead of yourself.

You can do this.

The pacing is intended to slow you down, and offer up daily practices so you can fully embody each step of the Code before moving onto the next.

Don't let the simplicity of these steps fool you. They are powerful, decisive and transformative. We are learning the truth about clutter and coming into mind-body awareness in order to have compassion for ourselves, not to make life a living hell. There are no scare tactics here, only love. We can't clear clutter if we're so fearful that we don't even begin.

Stay disciplined on this journey of ten weeks, do every experiment down to the minute. The steps are simple, but the results are profound.

If it seems boring, do it anyway. If it seems trivial, do it anyway. If it seems stupid, do it anyway. If it seems tiresome, do it anyway.

Invest in yourself. You deserve this.

We have to give ourselves time to clear away the caked on dirt from our lenses. It took us this long to acquire all the clutter; let's give ourselves time to clear it away. Insight and awareness await us if we allow the distractions time to evaporate from view.

Don't rush the time devoted to nurturing and caring for yourself. This is for your transformation. Why race through it?

THE 10 STEPS

Be willing to try.

If applicable, please consult your physician before working through the Declutter Code as there are some physical activities suggested. Use your intuition to guide you through these experiments so that, above all, you stay in good health. Your best gauge is how you feel. If you do get sick or get emotional during this, just know there is a lot of release happening with these experiments; allow your body to cleanse itself. A weak mind might be trying to convince your body that it is not strong enough to handle this process. What do you believe?

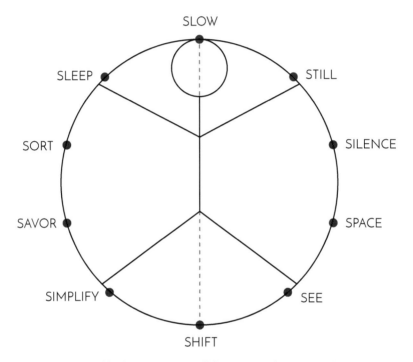

Uniting mind and body, encompassing all that we are, is the energy of the 10 steps.

slow

Smile, breathe and go slowly.
−THICH NHAT HANH

To *slow* is to pause. It is a significant and noticeable pausing to breathe, notice and reflect. Slowing down is taking our foot off the gas, and physically slowing the movement of our bodies. It is becoming slow to speak, slow to react.

It invites in a respite from the frantic, crazed *doing*. A treat for our sanity. We are slowing down to go with the flow.

To slow is to come into awareness because as we slow down physically and mentally, our senses heighten. And because we slow down, our surroundings slow down. The slower pace makes it possible to hear, smell, see, taste and touch, more consciously, more mindfully.

When our minds and bodies calm and slow down, we can more easily tap in to mind-body awareness. We can differentiate form from Feeling, so we're not as quick to give something meaning and turn it into an object. We're slower to react, more attentive to what's coming in through our senses.

How It Clears Clutter

Slowing is decluttering. Constant movement clutters the mind. It doesn't allow for a break in the monotony of hustle and routine, which can lead to overwhelm and overload. The more cool, calm and collected we become, the easier it is to slow the clutter build-up at inception.

Slowing down is slowing our mental activity from missile-launcher to mindful. We become watchful over our thoughts and stories. We deliberately slow our intake of information, being more cautious over our ears, eyes and mouths. And what results is being slower to judge, complain, and victimize ourselves. Slower to stuff our mouths with food for comfort or escape. Slower to fill our calendars with too many activities and appointments to hide behind busyness.

When we slow, we build in breathing room—room for rest and reflection. Space opens in our schedules and our day-to-day routine to live and experience what's happening now, instead of five minutes from now. Last-minute activities are few and far between. Planning our day around our priorities and resources comes easier. Rushing around stops being as necessary or important.

When we slow down, we make time to experience deeply and fully, which makes space for observation and gratitude. Allowance and acceptance. We're slower to draw conclusions or make assumptions. We're slower to commit to new roles and responsibilities. We pause for inspiration before acting.

By slowing down, we begin to balance the agenda of both spirit-mind and body-mind. The Truth penetrates through our clutter, down to our core, making the access to spirit easier and easier, clearer and clearer. More and more a belief. More and more of a behavior and a way of life.

So, not always on the run, we're scheduling room to breathe in our life experience. We're able to measure our activities against our priorities and see if they're aligned. If they're not aligned, we're slow (not frantic) enough to make proper adjustments to our day without huge hiccups.

What This Feels Like

The benefits of slowing down are endless, starting with how it makes us feel. Slowing feels like the physiological slowing down of breath, pulse and heart rate. Slowing feels like a calmer mind and body.

It feels like the mind slowing its barrage of thought. It feels like relief from the constant grind of going and doing, doing and going. It feels like "taking a breather."

Slowing down heightens the senses so we are more keenly aware of even the most subtle thought, smell, texture, sound and flavor. Attuned to our surroundings, all senses work jointly to offer a robust experience. The sniffing nose smells a single fragrance in a bouquet. The touching hand feels the smallest pebble in the sand. The listening ear hears the faintest chord in the orchestra. The tasting mouth tastes the hint of nutmeg in a bowl of chili.

A Tool for Slowing

Yoga is a great tool for mind-body awareness. And mind-body awareness is pivotal in decluttering. Yoga, with its strengthening and lengthening postures, helps us slow down and connect mind with body. To get into a posture and gradually perfect its expression within your body requires our slowing down and an intention to adjust the body accordingly. Mind sets the pace and the endurance of the body. Slow, deliberate movement allows us to recognize the interplay between mind and body and how they constantly work as one. Each yogic posture depends on every muscle group, for balance, for execution, and the mind is at the precipice of each. We can witness how the mind thinks and gets us to move. With the focus you harness moving through each posture, you touch your insides.

Yoga is working to engage the body and still the mind so there is no distraction to peace. Peace falls over us as we choose to focus the mind on our mat. While the body-mind is occupied with slow, deliberate bodily movement, the spirit-mind is free to observe our thinking. This is moving meditation. We *mind* our thoughts and gain insight as to how they affect the body's behavior.

When I first got into yoga, I immediately felt the mind-body connection that it fosters. I'd watch myself move from one posture into the next and felt the ripple effect throughout my body. I found that whenever I fell out of a posture or got discouraged, I could immediately sense that it was because of what I was telling myself in the posture. I'd be comparing myself to another yogi. I'd be dissatisfied with my abilities or progress. I'd be hungry, looking forward to what I was going to eat after class. Distractions. And in those moments my practice suffered. I'd fall out of a balancing posture. I wouldn't stretch as far in Forward Fold. I'd collapse in my headstands.

Now, when I am focused on the postures, on the instruction and on my breath, I am tuned into the inner workings of my mind and how it creates my entire life experience. I can stay focused. Distractions that come aren't as derailing, surprises aren't as shocking. As a result, I begin to feed my body encouraging and motivating words. I begin to love on myself in and out of class.

Experiment
Week 1

Slowing down is the first step in becoming mindful. And for that reason, it's important to note that the Declutter Code rests on this first step primarily. Slowing, pausing to breathe, is chief among the ten steps.

This week, focus on slowing down. Spend each day slowing down. Slowing the mind and slowing the body go hand in hand. Over the next seven days, experiment with a slower approach to your day.

Your game plan for the next seven days:

1. There's a time to run and a time to walk. This week, walk. Stop rushing around convinced you need the adrenaline rush to calm your nerves. Instead, do the opposite of feeding that adrenaline. Walk instead of run as your morning workout. Breathe with strong lungs, naturally, instead of gasping for air as you walk for 20-30 minutes. Swing your arms with each stride for extra oxygen to your heart.
2. Stop rushing to meetings. Leave the house 15 minutes earlier than you need to, just so you can get there with time to sit, read and contemplate before your appointment. Allow at least a five-minute buffer for yourself to regroup and refocus from the previous task. And breathe.
3. Do not text and drive. If you've done exercises 1 and 2, whatever you have to say can wait until you're sitting, waiting for your next appointment.
4. Take a beginner *Hatha*, *vinyasa* or *Ashtanga* yoga class, even if you're a seasoned pro. Return to the basics of a beginner yoga class so you can slow down. Watch your mind instruct your body. Watch how both work in unison. Come into a beginner's mind to experience the connecting of mind and body without heavily contorting postures or inversions. You can find a local yoga studio simply by searching "yoga + *your city*" on Google. I would attend a group class for your first time, if you can, for the benefit of live instruction. Most studios offer a free first class.

Watch your thoughts as you experiment this week. Are your thoughts encouraging or discouraging as you slow down? Do you feel like even your thinking has slowed? Do you feel like you're wasting time slowing down, or are you finding peace in the slower action?

still

Be still and know.

-PSALM 46:10

To *still* is to calm through non-action. Like a lake calms after a ripple, stilling allows everything to settle—centering toward the True Self. Without disruption, the mind, like the lake's sand below, calms and returns home.

Stillness is a magic potion, if you ask me. A panacea. It is centering and calming, and it settles the mind's needle north on our compass.

What is it for us to be *still*? It means we stop all activity—physically and mentally—and just sit with what is. Sit still with what is happening now. Sit still as the minutes tick by. Sit still with thoughts as they come and go. Sit still with the body as it twitches and itches. Sit still with the painful or pleasurable sensations. And do nothing. Make no effort to respond or react. Just let what is happening, happen. Let what is being, be.

The more we allow beingness, the more we are able to consciously decipher between conscious and unconscious action.

Calming the mind in this way prepares us for insight. It shows up in the stillness, in the allowing. Stay open and receptive in the still moment and allow life to happen.

Stilling frees us from the need to move, and gives us permission to *be.*

The mind, settled, sees beyond this world and into the great unknown, into spirit consciousness. Knowing we can settle and be still is a gift to the senses, giving them the unhindered access to the world. The glimpses of freedom are enough to convince us that there's more to life than what we see here on the earth's rocky floor.

How It Clears Clutter

To still the body is to declutter. This step continues the decluttering process by calming the storm of clutter. Halting all movement and activity helps us to begin the decluttering process internally and externally by settling the stormy waters, calming the chaos, smoothing the friction. As we still, we drastically slow the clinging to new clutter, and with no more clutter being added, it's easier to see what clutter already exists that we've been turning a blind eye to. It's easier to see what's underneath the stuff that we pile on to overcompensate or make a name for ourselves, inventing an identity to use in the world.

In stilling, we're stilling the forming of new mental concepts. We're gathering what's already formed and holding it for reassessment.

Finding stillness in the body is the ultimate retreat because by first stilling the physical body, the mind is free to follow. When you stop the moving and the fidgeting, your mind can calm and settle, detaching from the need to *do*. We allow what is happening around us to happen without our involvement.

Relaxation in the body is like acceptance in the mind. We accept what is. Without having to *do*, we don't seek to change, alter, avoid or deny.

When we still, we come into presence because there's nowhere else to be except here, now. We get a taste of peace. We stop needing to be everywhere else and we choose to be right here, attending to right now. And in this moment there is us, naked, thoughtful, vulnerable.

What This Feels Like

Stilling feels like settling and calming mind and body. Mind relaxes away from demands and expectations. Body relaxes away from activity and busyness.

Stilling feels like coming into the here and now simply by shutting off the need to move in order to distract ourselves from going deep within. We can't begin to clear the clutter if we don't first turn inward.

To still ourselves feels like inviting peace into our entire being. There's no obstruction in the form of movement or obligation or demands or thoughts of having to be anywhere else but here, now.

Stilling feels like turning our attention inward. With our body still, the mind can begin to still and come to center, opening our mind's eye. As we feel ourselves veering in directions other than north, we can adjust the associations that keep us resisting the flow.

A Tool for Stilling

I am so grateful for meditation. Since I started meditating a few years out of college, it has helped me in ways I can't put into words. Meditation is the process of disciplining our minds. It is coming into active vigilance over our mind's thoughts and our body's movements. Like in Step 1, we use yoga as our tool, but now we incorporate meditation (*Dhyana*), one of the eight Yoga Sutras. *Asana,* which means "to sit down," is our posture of choice in Step 2. By stilling our bodies to meditate, we grow in concentration, insight and clarity. *Sitting meditation* cultivates our conscious mind's eye and enables us to discern form from Feeling.

The more we discipline ourselves to sit still and meditate, the easier the act of stilling becomes any time we need to restore inner peace. Meditation dilutes overwhelm and chaos in the mind, loosens habitual mindsets, clears sabotaging beliefs. It does this by drawing the mind's attention to one thought at a time—a sensation, word, mantra, even the rhythm of the breath. By training our mind to attend to this one thought, we quickly see how often we are pulled from that thought on to others. Witnessing endless amounts of thoughts coming and going, we can recognize our thoughts as fickle, flighty and completely innocuous. Nothing permanent about them and nothing harmful.

So as we watch our thoughts and discipline our minds to go back to the chosen word or mantra, we can see how easy it would be to allow thoughts to come and go like clouds, floating by us while we remain still. Those thoughts can't phase us or sway us from our seated foundation—which is why the disciplined stilling of meditation itself is so important. We can see how easy it would be to choose not to turn these thoughts into form by clinging and hoarding them. With this insight now being honed in meditation, we can take it into our daily life and choose not to make form from Feeling.

Among countless psychological and physiological benefits, meditation cultivates equanimity, compassion and unity. In our stillness, we settle enough to see that we humans are all the same—all cluttered, overloaded, fearful—which softens our hearts for everyone as for ourselves. We connect easier with people because we're all facing the same challenge of cluttered minds convincing us we're inferior or unlovable. We grow in insight into the human predicament: fear.

We start to see ourselves at the helm of our rafts, able to steer back into flow whenever we decide.

Experiment
Week 2

This week focus on stilling mind and body. Sit with no agenda, no TV, no distractions. Deliberately take up a posture with complete consciousness and awareness. Pay attention to what you are doing—when you start and when you stop. Relax into stillness.

This week begins our meditation practice. The benefits of meditation are in the discipline and consistency of your practice. Give yourself time to meditate and break away from the day-to-day routine. Sit quietly with yourself, without action, and you will reap unfathomable rewards in your clarity and inner peace.

Just like the best money advice is to pay yourself first at least 10% of your income, I recommend we give to ourselves a moment's peace first thing every morning. Feed your spirit-mind first with meditation. Give yourself some "me" time, not doing what others mandate you to do, but what you choose to do to declutter your mind.

If you meditate two hours a day or if you have never meditated at all, start there. Where you are is perfect. The meditation advised in this book starts at two minutes in duration for those who aren't meditating at all and need a starting point. Don't go into it expecting drastic changes immediately. That is a sure-fire way to quit before you even start. If you already meditate, feel free to use your current meditation time, adding on as the weeks progress.

Your game plan for the next seven days:

1. Set your alarm to wake up 15 minutes earlier than you normally would. Once awake in the morning, use two of these new, waking minutes to meditate. Get quiet and close your eyes. Relax into stillness by sitting down comfortably with your back erect. Focus on the mantra, or phrase: "I am still" and push aside disrupting thoughts in exchange for these three words. Let other thoughts come and go like clouds, always returning to your mantra: I am still. Repeat the mantra quietly to yourself, over and over during these two minutes. Whenever you drift to the thoughts of yesterday or plans for the day, stop and return to your mantra: **I am still.** Do this without interruption for two full minutes.

2. Lie down on the ground, on your back and be still (*Shivasana*, or Corpse Pose). If this hurts your back, you can bend your knees upward with your feet flat on the earth. Just lie there, prostrate, surrendering to nothingness. You can set your alarm for a few minutes, or you can allow your body to indulge and take however long it wants. When your body and mind are ready to awaken and rise, you will. Wait for that time until you move.

3. The calmer you are inside, the more you can see how the serene stillness of our surroundings carries an indescribable beauty. Go outside and sit comfortably in the shade, on the grass or in a hammock. Still the body. Notice any area in the body that can soften. Use your body's stillness to stare into space, stare at gardens, stare at your surroundings to notice what is still and beautiful. Notice what doesn't need to move and how beautiful it is. Use the stillness of the body to allow the mind to still. Observe. Do not make sense of it, do not make it important, do not try to explain it.

4. Still your tongue this week. Give into nonaction for the mouth. When you are in conversation with others, stop and listen to their words. If you ask a question, listen instead of thinking about what you'll say when they are done answering. Wait until someone asks you what you're working on before you offer up all that's on your

plate. Wait to be invited into conversation before you chime in. Still your tongue and let your ears do most of the work this week. Take in the songs of everyday life all around you that don't require your vibrato. This will prepare you for Step 3.

As you go through these exercises, notice any floating thoughts that say, "I'm inferior," "I'm not good enough," or, "This isn't working." Don't let this inner-sabotage distract you from the goal of *discipline*. Work through any initial discouragement, frustration or boredom. Stick to your game plan, despite how weird it might seem.

3
silence

Turn off your mind. There is a place beyond thought that already knows—trust in that.

—RAM DAS

Silence is the absence of sound. It is the hushing of chatter and commotion, of song and speech. It's the muting of noise. It's the quieting of the mind.

Silence allows us to turn our focus inward. When we settle our surroundings, our body, then mind, our inner ears aren't as distracted. We can listen from within and hear our inner dialogue. Our thoughts don't have to compete with much else to be heard.

When we silence externally and internally, restless thoughts of wonder and insecurity may still drone on, but as white noise in the background, and with a much lower volume.

The more we soften our thoughts, give in to the silence and derive comfort from noiselessness, we will experience a growth in awareness and an increased ease to decluttering.

How It Clears Clutter

Silencing is decluttering. Silence is choosing what we listen to. We don't have to listen to anything we don't want to. By actively listening only to what we choose, we can monitor the intake of information. We can choose to listen to the silence. The inside chatter eventually gets drowned out by the peace of silence and the intermittent thoughts of observation.

In silence, bodily senses sharpen. We can attend to ourselves. Hearing is turned inward to hear our inner dialogue, how we talk to ourselves and what we say. Like how without alcohol, the liver is free to detox and rest. We do the same type of cleansing when we stop the senses from overactivity and free the mind to attend to itself, listen to itself, cleanse itself.

Too rarely do we allow for this silence to notice how loud our inner dialogue is and what it's saying. We're too busy filling our time with distracting noise.

Silence is healing for the mind because we're lessening the intake of information. We're pausing the media and the conversations. When we're not hearing from everything going on outside, we can begin to turn our attention to the noise coming from inside.

It may be difficult to silence the mind completely and, actually, I don't know anyone who can. There's always something floating around in there. But the point is to *near* silence. How quiet can you get? Ultimately, we strive for the balance of soundlessness with sound. While it might not always seem doable, sometimes just the removal of outside chatter can help curb the overwhelming inside chatter.

When we've mastered silence, thoughts that serve to distract or disempower come fewer and farther between. They'll float by like clouds and eventually will dissipate and disappear. Lowering the volume on inner chatter enables us to have more quiet moments, where the noises don't *matter* enough to throw us off.

What This Feels Like

Silence feels like inviting in noiselessness, inside and outside. It feels like loosening the ties that keep us tethered to sound—the need to talk and hear. The need to hear what might make us feel better, the need to say what others want to hear.

As we move through Step 3, we feel the mutiny of thought already slowing and settling. By now, silence is a welcomed state. Joining slowness and stillness with silence feels like a break from the chaos. Sometimes, the cure to our mental overwhelm lies in spending a few moments in these first three steps.

Mastering the joy of silence feels like true peace, because mind and body are still functioning to keep us alive, but we are no longer chasing, seeking or overcompensating. We feel content with who and what we are, when and where we are. Silence is feeling content in your own skin, happy to be you in your own company.

A Tool for Silencing

Your breath is the perfect tool for silence. It's always there, whether you're aware of it or not. It sustains you. It comforts you. It calms you.

Every cell in our bodies uses oxygen to live. The breath is very cleansing. As we inhale we take in clean, fresh oxygen. Taking a moment to breathe deeply to calm ourselves, to rejuvenate ourselves. Clear out all the gunk and blockages that keep us from being fully present in this moment.

We can't see breath, most times don't even feel it if we're in our normal trance of everyday life, but we keep on breathing instinctually. To actually notice and feel breath going in and out of your lungs, filling you, nourishing you, energizing you, knowing it's what keeps you alive, that's to be present. That's us witnessing an everyday miracle, our breath working on our behalf.

We can witness the same thing about the universe, about the divine. Anytime you feel overcome with gratitude, wrapped in love, or taken over in laughter, that's your firsthand experience of the divine working in your life, and as easy to see as noticing your breath. God works through us, for us and as us just as our breath moves through us, for us, as us.

Breath, since we rarely think about it, prevent it from coming, or make a big deal about it, represents flow. Breathing is *going with the flow*.

If we were to suffocate ourselves, we wouldn't be able to breathe; we'd be cut off from our lifeline. This is analogous to suffocating ourselves with clutter. We suffocate ourselves, our dreams, our aspirations, our loved ones, or we let someone else suffocate us. That's us clinging to a sinking anchor, preventing growth and forward momentum. We complain and we decide "it's unfair." We stifle ourselves with mind-made problems.

But we breathe and we untie stomach knots, loosen strongholds and soften tension. Breath symbolizes releasing our grip on *stuff*. Releasing our fixations, obsessions and habits.

I love sitting silently with my breath and practicing *Pranayama*, which is the conscious controlling of inhalations and exhalations. (It's not recommended to do this without a coach as it can be dangerous.) Returning to the simple things, like breath, reminds me to turn inward (inhale) and let go (exhale). Let go of tension, let go of anxiety. Whenever I get anxious, I'll close my eyes and take three big, deep, lung-filling breaths. I find that it regulates my heart rate, it settles my erratic thoughts and, most importantly, it centers my attention toward the ease of the moment. I'm reminded not to complicate things.

How we do one thing is how we do everything. How we attend to the most basic, purest part of ourselves—like allowing for refreshing moments of solitude and silence—speaks of how well we attend to all aspects of our well-being.

Breath as a tool for silencing is effective because we can silence all other noise to just tune into the sound of the breath. Always there, always humming. Even when we're silent, the breath and the rant of the mind stay. After the clutter is cleared, this is what remains.

Experiment
Week 3

Let this week be about silencing. Turn it off, lower the volume, do whatever it takes to bring about more silence around you.

Your game plan for the next seven days:

1. Increase the time in sitting meditation in the morning by one minute. So if you were sitting for two minutes last week, sit for three minutes each morning this week. Your new mantra for this week's meditation will be, "I appreciate silence." Repeat it quietly to yourself, over and over during this time. When your mind wanders, return your attention to your mantra: **I appreciate silence**.

2. Go this week not listening to anything on the commute to and from work. This includes when you're headed to client meetings or to run errands. Sit with the sound of the car, the road and your own thoughts. If you work from home, or have kids in the car on your commute, spend 30 minutes in the morning in complete silence—no talking or ambient noise. Then again in the evening, 30 minutes of silence.

3. Take a mass media break this week. This means turning off the "opinion" noise. No TV, news radio, talk radio, YouTube videos, podcasts, social media, blogs, or anything else you would categorize as such. What we want to stay away from this week is persuasion, propaganda and other people's agendas. We want to return to what matters to us, to what we *feel* instead of outside opinions. It might take filtering out a few outspoken distractions and interruptions before we hear our own broadcast blaring on the loudspeaker—what we couldn't hear before because we were too concerned with what everyone else was saying.

4. To return to the breath is to return to that place of divinity inside us. This is how we refuel and reset our awareness. Turn all senses to the breath, its sound, its texture. Its volume; listen to it. Allow it to be the only sound you hear. Be one with it. Embody it as it moves oxygen through your body, in and out of your lungs. Focusing on the breath occupies the mind and gives it a focal point for its attention. When we're aware of where our attention is at any point, that's presence.

This week, sit with the sound of your breath. For one minute before you go to bed this week, make it a point to listen for your breath amidst all other sounds. As you do this, alternate between breathing out of your nose and then out of your mouth. Play with the length of each inhalation and each exhalation. Play with the texture of it. Play with the volume of it. Play with holding it for a few seconds before releasing it. Notice it move your belly. Feel it exit your nose. And when those outside noises arise, airplanes flying, people talking, sirens blaring, toys squeaking, seek out the sound of your barely audible breath. Return to it.

Deepak Chopra, author of *The Seven Spiritual Laws of Success*, says, "In the silence we hear the truth and know the solutions." In the silence, we find all we need to find and know all we need to know. It's there for us, within us. We just have to listen.

Watch your mind as you experiment with your game plan this week. When everything around you is quiet, where do your thoughts go?

4

space

Between stimulus and response there is a space.
In that space is our power to choose our response.
In our response lies our growth and our freedom.

–VIKTOR E. FRANKL

Space is the distance between two things. In this case, it refers to the space between sense and thought, thought and story, story and behavior. Increasing the space from thought to behavior naturally delays our reactivity as if to make time to think of not reacting at all.

We use the space to lower our voices, to come off the ledge, to subdue our tempers. We use the space to tell different stories, to choose a different thought.

Space makes room for new perspectives, because we're open enough to receive new insight (Step 5). And, more importantly, the expanding space allows for patience and presence in order to hear this insight.

Also in this step, we're creating space, or distance, between sensation and object. Enough to discern which is which. In the space, we can allow Feeling (hearing, smelling, seeing, tasting, touching) to stand alone—clear of labels and definitions. In the space, we can spot the cause of our problems, the cause of our habits and the cause of our *dis-ease*. We recognize the make-believe and our imaginary drama.

The emptiness that space provides gives us access to conscious awareness, the innate knowing that's always within reach.

How It Clears Clutter

Space is the absence of clutter. A void that sometimes feels awkward because we're so used to filling the space with monologue, possessions and worry. But in accepting space, we free ourselves to live more peacefully in that void of stuff, needing things less and less for comfort. Eventually we relish in the continued expansion of space in and around us. We find that we naturally build spaciousness in our minds, hearts, home and office.

Space reminds us we're in this world, but not of this world.

Open, clear minds clear all clutter because of the honed awareness. Space offers perspective.

When you open your mind to the possibilities, forgiveness comes easier because we don't expect everyone to think like and act like we do. We're free from expectations, allowing space for our own judgments to fall away before we start deciding on requirements for other people. Judgment forms less often because the space between observation and judgment expands, so much so that judgment rarely has a chance to form.

Consider this like a highway with a ton of traffic. Road rage, flared tempers, impatient drivers. As we're driving, we are so close to the car ahead of us that when tempers flare, we're quick to react, slam on our brakes, yell out the window and throw up the middle finger. Fender-benders, pile-ups.

Now consider the opposite of that. No traffic on the road, plenty of space between cars ahead and behind. The ride is smooth, the drive is enjoyable. When someone ahead of you hits their brakes, we gradually take our foot off the gas, no need for braking because there's plenty of room before you even near their bumper. You have time to notice their brake lights, release your gas pedal and consider a lane change. No one's in harm's way, no one's getting hurt from an abrupt slam on the brakes. No one is rear-ended. We are free to slow down, pause. Before absolutely needing to hit our brakes, there's time to assess the scene, find alternatives, and then return to our original speed as the person ahead begins to move on as before. No judgment, no reactions, just calm, easy movement.

The more distance we allow between stimulus and reaction, the freer we become because we're allowing life to unfold without our resistance. We break from the clinging, the impulses, the defensiveness, because there's time to sit back, watch and observe. And in that seat of witness, we find peace.

We can also put space between thought and belief. Not every mental concept has to be molded into a belief. Thoughts can float by while we observe from a distance, choosing just to watch. With space, we have enough of a clear vantage point to let thoughts pass as clouds pass in the sky.

What This Feels Like

Space feels like spaciousness. It feels like making room to relax, rest and regroup. It feels like time to process, consider and ponder, rather than assume, judge or jump to conclusions. It feels like room to consider perspectives other than your own to discover alternative explanations, alternative realities.

When we step away from "my way" and open ourselves up to "a way," it feels like enlightenment. It feels like equanimity and neutrality, where everything will be ok either way because we have the space to recognize it without fears and projections. We're not directly affected by everything because we have a buffer from which to observe everything from afar. Clarity opens our eyes to see life as an experience to appreciate, not a catastrophe to dread. Everything can be as it is, come as it will, and we'll be ok.

Space feels like breathing room. Time. Growth. Expansion. It feels like the openness to stretch mind and body. To welcome new mindsets. To make way for new possibilities. To accept new realities.

A Tool for Creating Space

A daily journal is a great way to create space. Writing your thoughts cleanses stress from the mind—gets it out of our heads and onto paper, making mental space for the present moment. We write down the regrets of yesterday so we don't bring them into today. We write down our fears about tomorrow so we can live right now.

The best thing about journaling is the freedom of the blank page. You can write anything on these private pages knowing they'll never tell. Flow freely on paper because this is your time and this is the place to do so. Disclose your worries, your concerns, your joys and your triumphs. And the pages will reveal your patterns, your fears and your solutions. Journaling helps us get to the root of these mental concepts so we see how we're creating our own problems. With that insight, we can watch the clutter begin to lose its power over us.

I journal every day. Sometimes it is to recap the day before. Sometimes it is complaining and whining about my current predicament. Sometimes it is *visioning*, where I envision my goals and how it will feel to reach them. In visioning, I get to embody a new story and those sensory experiences that serve to call that reality closer to me. The more I live in Feelings I want to feel, the more those Feelings come to stay. I enjoy daydreaming and telling stories because I'm a creative person, so I can't help it! It opens me up to creating my own future.

Journaling also helps us play out scenarios in our minds, like if we're dealing with disgruntled employees or an inconsiderate spouse. We can script out our role in it all, discovering what we could do differently. Because we don't know what the best or worst outcome could possibly be from our limited vantage point, we stay open. We only see what we think we see, what we think is happening now, and we interpret it however makes sense given our most recent understanding of things. Journaling will reveal this.

After a few weeks of journaling, chances are we'll see the same story repeated over and over, the same fears, the same joys. With it all out on paper, we have the space to come out from under the rubble.

Experiment
Week 4

Use this week to put some space between you and people, you and work, you and your busy schedule. The space will allow time for self-reflection and self-discovery.

Also, your sitting meditation time is increasing and you're likely getting discouraged or feeling like by the end of this you're sitting for too long. Just trust the process and allow yourself these ten weeks of transformation. After these few weeks, you can go back to life as usual (if you still want to).

Your game plan for the next seven days:

1. Increase your morning sitting meditation by one minute this week, so you'll sit for four minutes every morning this week if you were sitting for three minutes before. Let your mantra for this week be,

"I make space." Repeat it quietly to yourself, over and over during this time. When your mind wanders, return your attention to your mantra: **I make space.**

2. Build in time for yourself this week, a space of at least 30 minutes, to do whatever you want—but do it alone. Put it in your calendar and don't deviate from it. Some ideas: roam the garden, walk around downtown, go see a movie, make dinner reservations for one, read a book in the park.

3. Put time between what happens and what your mind tells you to do about it (your reaction). We think 60,000 thoughts a day, many of them triggering a habitual response. This week, for seven days straight, whenever you experience something, give yourself 10 minutes before you make a reactive move (unless you're saving a life!). For example, when hungry, tired or angry, give yourself 10 minutes before you send that angry email, write it then delete it. Before you order unhealthy food, drink eight ounces of water instead. Before climbing into bed, meditate. Give yourself time between the trigger and the mindless habit.

4. You'll need a pen and notebook for this one. Nothing special, just a bound notebook with several blank pages and a pen that works. We're going to journal for five minutes without interruption every morning this week. Write about your life, your desires, your fears. Write down everything. Get it out of your mind onto paper. The intention is to clear the mind and make space for presence. Trap your thoughts, worries, concerns and plans for the day, and journal them onto paper, handwritten! Then leave the journal at home as you go about your day.

With space, there is recognition of question and answer, cause and effect. As you go about this week, ask yourself, "Can I see this differently?" "Do I have to look at it this way?" Journal your answers.

see

We do not see things as they are, we see them as we are.

−THE TALMUD

The fifth step, *see*, is to see with full awareness, full sensory awareness. It is seeing purely. We are able to recognize form from Feeling, Truth from illusion. We recognize thoughts exactly as they are: harmless mental concepts.

The sensation of sight embraces all that comes through the gateway of eyes and mind with composure and unbiased receptivity.

Seeing is sensing without story. In this step, we see without needing to explain what we see. Instead, we can appreciate what we take in through our eyes without making it something it's not (nonsense). We can appreciate what we see, understanding that we're projecting our internal state onto that which we see.

Seeing, in this context, could also be labeled "insight" (seeing inside) because we come from a place of knowing that we see things based on how we see ourselves. We know that what we see is being interpreted through our lenses, our perspective, subject to our moods, our labels and our beliefs.

We see ourselves in the clutter.

Once we know that our worldview is a projection of what's happening internally, we're free to work on ourselves, being the change we wish to see in the world. We're no longer pointing the finger away from us, but rather back in our direction. We are responsible for what we see and how we see it. We're no longer victims.

How It Clears Clutter

Seeing is to see *through* clutter. The previous step prepared us the space to gain a vantage point from a distance. From there, we bring about a new perspective. That new perspective allows us to decipher what thoughts beget what behavior. To see the effect of our thoughts. To really be open to perceiving differently, behaving differently, we have to see differently.

It's in seeing through clutter that we're able to recognize its fickle nature. When we recognize clutter as fickle and always changing form, we recognize that it's powerless without our thoughts. It's mind-made. We can change it at any time. When we see this truth, we aren't as susceptible to clutter's taunt, and therefore not as willing to hoard it. We open our eyes to its futility, serving only to keep us imprisoned in fear. With awareness, we break free.

Seeing, in this step, is seeing with that part of our mind that is connected to God and beyond this world. The more we operate from that vantage point, the wider our perspective grows. The bigger we allow ourselves and others to be. We're not as small or limited with our sight, we see more for ourselves, more peace, more clarity.

Seeing is clear seeing. Seeing with a conscious eye, without the inside clutter that blinds us to our greater Truth. Within the space we've cultivated, we can see with pure, unadulterated vision. We see from an observer state—taking it all in without casting judgment or forming biases. What we see is not subject to our conditions or control.

We're now willing to see with open, conscious eyes, no longer accepting the material world as the end-all. We remember we also exist in a realm far beyond this earthly plane, connected to the universal power surge, and so we turn our gaze toward Source. And because we always find what we look for, we continue to find evidence of that which keeps us connected and conscious.

What This Feels Like

Seeing feels like clear sight, or clarity. It feels like observation, recognition, appreciation. Acknowledging and appreciating what you see and how you see it. Seeing feels like seeing *through, into* and *within.* It feels like *looking responsibly,* meaning we take responsibility for what we see in the world because we understand it is a projection of what is going on inside.

Seeing feels like an enriching of the senses, enjoying their fullness and our aliveness. It feels like looking out into the vastness of the world and embracing every viewpoint without bias, judgment or self-pity. Seeing feels like a new experience created with new eyes to see and appreciate each new day. Seeing is acceptance. It is recognizing things as they are without having to make them different. Allowance. Allowing what is to be as it is. Without makeup, without costume, without blindfolds. It is growth toward what is occurring now. Presence.

A Tool for Seeing

A mirror is our tool for seeing, both mentally and physically. A mirror reflects ourselves back to us. What we see in this mirror is what we are willing to see. The mind interpreted a sensory message and spit out a reflection. This reflection tells us what's going on inside, just like a bathroom mirror tells us what's showing up outside.

Each person we meet is a mirror for us—a reflection of our projection. Since we are always projecting our own mental concepts onto others, we see the world as *we* are. And how we see that person is representative of what we think about ourselves.

Even when the "reflection" comes from someone else's lens, we still detect ourselves in their vision. Sometimes outside eyes (family, a coach, mentor, or friend) help us see what we've been denying we see.

When we're blinded by clutter, we don't accept change or unexpected surprises—especially if they're not what we planned for or built a schedule around. We expect everything to go just as we think it *should*. But what if how it *should* happen isn't how it *would* happen if we allowed what *could* happen?

We don't really know what *should* happen because we don't know what *could* happen. Perspective determines our outlook and, depending on our outlook, the world is limited or limitless. When we blind ourselves to all the possible *could-happens*, we don't see all the opportunity in what does happen. We can't control what happens, only how we choose to see what does.

Experiment
Week 5

Spend this week opening your eyes to newness. Embrace the differences around you by taking them in with your eyes and then into your mental awareness. Appreciate the refreshing quality they bring to your view of the world.

Your game plan for the next seven days:

1. Increase your sitting meditation time by one minute this week. So every morning, you'll sit for five minutes if you began this journey at two minutes. Let your mantra be, "I see with open eyes." Repeat it quietly to yourself, over and over during this time. When your mind wanders, return your attention to your mantra: **I see with open eyes**.

2. Whenever you find yourself judging another person, try to stop yourself and come up with something nice to say. Turn this nice statement into a compliment and tell it to their face. When you compliment others, you open your eyes to how true the statement is. It becomes true for you. And when it becomes true, you start to notice that those same things you complimented in others are in you.

3. Let friends and family know you are staying away from gossip this week and won't participate in those types of conversations. Ask them to hold you accountable by not letting you listen or contribute. Protect yourself from these certain influences this week. If you do enter a gathering where this is the nature of the discussion, kindly excuse yourself and immediately exit the conversation. Don't stick around.

4. Each morning, look in a full-length mirror at yourself, preferably naked, and point out all the things you see on your body that you appreciate. List out loud three things, from the beauty mark on your nose to your long, strong legs. Utilize all senses as you point out what you love and admire about your appearance. Show gratitude for it by placing a hand there, breathing adoration straight into that area. Smile as you do this. Do not say anything disparaging or belittling, even if for a small chuckle. We are shifting away from those powerless thoughts. Besides, that's just more hiding behind words and facades.

As you move through this week's game plan, what new opportunities, possibilities and wisdom open up? Do you detect any non-truths that you've been clinging to, such as "I'm so pitiful," "I'm so unloveable," "I'm so incapable of peace and prosperity"? How can you see yourself differently in order to change that dialogue?

shift

You never have to change what you see,
only the way you see it.
—THADDEUS GOLAS, LAZY MAN'S
GUIDE TO ENLIGHTENMENT

To *shift* is to move or change over some distance. It is depth and openness to see in a new way, from a new vantage point. It's choosing to replace one paradigm for another, one belief for another, one point of view for another.

It's shifting our attention away from form and toward formlessness. It's shifting from attachment toward freedom. These subtle shifts can happen all day, with each decision we make.

Every moment, we bring with us a perspective. That perspective is the lens through which we view the world. It's an attitude or viewpoint about a particular subject or object (person, place or thing). The clearer this lens is, the clearer life becomes. The easier it becomes to shift our steps toward peace.

So in this step of shifting, we're choosing to step out of chaos and into peace. We're choosing clarity over confusion.

How It Clears Clutter

Shifting is conscious choosing. Every moment, we're at choice. We have the ability to choose our thoughts, our stories, our mood and our behavior. When we shift to a thought that is easy and empowering, we steer our raft back in flow. We're not resisting the flow, rather, we're moving with it. Clutter falls away from a raft going with the flow. Peace returns.

Now that we have space in which to shift, and the eyes to bring new perspective, we can shift our thoughts, beliefs, mood and behavior toward being compassionate, empowering, joyful and kind. When we shift, we deliberately choose *different*. Perhaps we need to shift in order to feel better, exchanging a pessimistic mood for an optimistic one. This is possible because it's as if we see from a new understanding. We've been enlightened and can no longer act from that old place.

When we shift beliefs, opinions and mindsets, our whole life shifts to take on a new light. Our lens is clear and we're clear-headed. We begin to respond from that place. And with that subtle change, we shift our entire life experience.

When we step into conscious choosing, we create a reality that is enjoyable. One that is fruitful. One that aligns our to-do lists with our priorities. We're not struggling to make it, for example, because we're attracting income from a place of service and value. Our perspective shifts toward openness and acceptance. We become aware enough to choose life, limitlessness and love over loss, limitation and lack.

We can shift toward empowering beliefs and lifestyles. When we're grateful for something, we get more to be grateful for. When we are generous, others are generous with us. Like a domino effect.

What This Feels Like

Shifting feels like moving from one thought to another, from one belief to another. It feels like creativity and innovation, coming up with different ideas, different outlooks, ideas, possibilities, and allowing each one to play itself out. It feels like taking a different approach and welcoming a different outcome.

Shifting feels like altering our perspective or outlook on life. It feels like having a change of heart. Like when you say no to a new project in favor of your priorities. When you start to work on a project and it doesn't feel congruent with where you are in life, you listen to that gut instinct and pass on the job. Or like when your best friend calls you up with sad news, rather than offering condolences, you offer support through quietly listening. When the time comes to speak, you console her with visions of a brighter tomorrow. You give her something to look forward to and get hopeful about, rather than contributing to her sadness.

Shifting feels like choosing a different response, like when you want to get angry, you think of how much worse it could be, and switch to understanding and compassion. Shifting is what's behind forgiveness and giving someone a second chance. It is easier to clean the slate when you're already conditioning yourself to think positive and welcome opportunity from a "bad" situation. It's easier to start fresh and begin again.

A Tool for Shifting

Use your mood for this one. Monitoring our mood helps us know when to shift from one belief to another, or wait to act on a certain thing because we're not in the right mental state. Mood is like a speedometer, letting us know if we're moving too fast and need to slow down. Or if we need to create some space from planning and do more living. If our mood is anxious, we might need to take a break and do some breathing exercises. If our mood is happy, we might need to live it up, soak in the moment and enjoy what's happening.

I consider my mood a gauge for what's going on with me deep inside. When I monitor my mood, I can see where my thoughts are or where they've gotten me as I was entranced in clutter (e.g. limiting beliefs). When I stop and recognize my mood, I can more easily shift toward a more empowering thought. Once I shift my perspective and mood to a lens of empowerment, compassion or gratitude, I start to see everything differently. Which means I can start to *act* from that place of empowerment, compassion or gratitude.

When I'm clear, I can choose my mood. When I'm not clear, choosing my mood seems impossible. But when I consciously put a peaceful smile on my face after getting sad news, I find that my mood slowly starts to follow. In a state of grief, the ability to smile doesn't seem as accessible. Yet all it takes is one small decision toward happiness and sadness begins to dissipate.

When we're depressed, we're choosing a downtrodden demeanor. We choose to stay in bed because that behavior seems most accessible when we're feeling hopeless. But with the power of the mind, we can get out of bed and put a skip in our step as soon as we make the decision to. If we need to gradually force a more hopeful mood before it becomes a natural mood, and that feels intentional to you, then try it. See what happens. What's it going to hurt? You're not forsaking a bad mood, you're just actively decluttering the lies that got you there.

When we're down and out, what's the most accessible mood that we can reach for that will leave us feeling slightly better? If we're in a bad mood, can we start to shift toward a better mood by changing our thoughts about the situation?

If you've gone through the first five steps, shifting now comes a lot easier. We've slowed down, stilled our bodies, quieted our minds, and made space to see the nature of our reality: thoughts form, nonstop, and create our world. A shift in your mood is a thought away. When you shift thought energy, you shift in belief and behavior. You can shift from a negative perspective to a positive one more easily. Your environment benefits from the brighter outlook. And those around you benefit from a happier you.

Experiment
Week 6

Spend this week shifting your perspective toward easy, empowering thoughts. Shift away from the discouraging thoughts that leave you feeling depleted. A new thought can be your way into a more empowered mindset. From negative, small and limiting beliefs, to positive, big and limitless beliefs. It can be shifting the way you look at yourself, and the image you have of your body or your personality. Or simply changing what you say and how you say it.

Shifting gets you from one state of mind to another. So what mood do you choose to have?

Your game plan for the next seven days:

1. Increase your sitting meditation time by one minute this week, so every morning you'll be sitting for at least six minutes. Let your mantra be, "I shift my thoughts toward peace." Repeat it quietly to yourself, over and over during this time. When your mind wanders, return your attention to your mantra: **I shift my thoughts toward peace.**

2. Keep a gratitude log this week, each day for these seven days. Every day, jot down five things you're grateful for, e.g. life, family, home, airplanes, flowers... Your list can repeat over the few days, but it's

sometimes more satisfying to think of a new set of five each day. Be sure to write down at least five things. You could write more than five, but no less. Challenge yourself, regardless of your mood, to come up with five things that you appreciate for making life a little sweeter.

3. For every negative thing you *think*, think two positive things about the same subject. Whenever you start to think negatively about someone, you'll want to immediately switch to thinking something positive about him. For every complaint that you *speak*, say out loud two positive things about the same subject. Clear the air of the negative comment by replacing it with two positive statements, leaving you and those around you with the echo of something more peaceful and loving.

4. Over the next few days, monitor your mood. Watch how you feel when you wake up, when you begin working, when you're around friends and family, and when you go to bed. Watch your level of re-activity in those moments. Try shifting your perspective even when it seems like the hardest thing to do. If someone cuts you in line, is there a story you can make up about that person that would make you feel compassionate toward their behavior? A great technique to practice compassion is to imagine yourself walking in the other person's shoes. We don't know what that person is telling himself or what stories he believes that makes him act that way. We don't know the battle he's fighting in his mind. Give him a pass.

In today's environment, it's easy to settle for chaos and confusion; it's all around you, everyone is suffering from it. Everyone's struggling in some way. So we revel in the company. But we can shift from fear toward empowerment with a simple shift in our perspective—and we can take everyone else with us when we do so.

Reflect on the quote at the start of this section. Is it easy to release your grudge toward an enemy and start being grateful to her for whatever good she brought into your life? Can you shift your focus to start looking for the good in that person, rather than the bad?

simplify

Life is really simple, but we insist on making it complicated.
—CONFUCIUS

To *simplify* is to remove the clutter that complicates and stains our lives. Simplicity is when life comes into balance and things relate more harmoniously. Harmony and peace are *simple*. When we simplify our lives, and chip away at clutter, we return to peace.

Life is easy. The minute we shift our thoughts to believe that, life rises to meet our faith. We start to see life get more manageable and we get more flexible—everything gets less chaotic.

Simplifying amounts to simple living. It leads to a clean home of warmth and love. A clean porch welcoming guests. A clean office with efficient systems. A clean fridge with fresh foods.

We were born into simplicity, but we complicate life when we resist the flow. The good news is, we can return to simple whenever we allow our raft to follow the current. We can return to our natural-born state.

How It Clears Clutter

"Again I say to you, it is easier for a camel to go through the eye of a needle, than for a rich man to enter the kingdom of God," Matthew 19:24. This Bible passage, to me, speaks of clutter. The rich man, with all his material wealth and larger-than-life personality, chases validation and legacy. If, in our lifetime, we chase only personalities and possessions, it's harder to return to simplicity (the kingdom of God, our eternal home) before we die.

The passage has nothing to do with being wealthy, per se. We can be very rich and still live a decluttered life. I interpret *rich* in that passage to mean *cluttered*—our clinging to possessions as opposed to living from Truth. Simplicity doesn't mean living meagerly, poor, or in a commune. It doesn't mean living with zero possessions and white walls. Our life will still carry a personality and some possessions as long as we inhabit these human bodies. All in all, it's what we cling to while in human form that represents our *clutterspace.*

Our cluttered minds have us thinking we need things outside of us for contentment. We don't need to chase outside for what we have inside, for what God has given us, for what remains when we leave this earth and return to our formless selves. We may not have the awareness yet to grasp this concept or see simplicity as possible, but all that means is that your need for stuff is greater than your trust that everything has already been provided. Like the "rich man," if we're stuck on the material concerns and possessions of the world, we're not clear enough to simplify. The "rich man" believes he needs those things to *make a living,* but that's cluttered thinking. He doesn't know the nature of his thoughts stand accountable in *making a life,* not how many sports cars he owns.

When we choose simplicity over material sustenance, material (matter) doesn't bog us down or keep us stuck. We recognize that we clutter our own lives by making people, places and things matter. But in that *knowing,* we are decluttering. We're not clinging, we're appreciating. From that place, we can begin to clean up our lives. We can make life simple again by not overtaxing ourselves with the drama, the unnecessary or the nonsense.

Simplifying is removing what we use to cover up our true selves. We hide behind stuff, personalities and costumes to divert the eyes. Or we speak unconsciously and banter nervously to divert the ears. We want to control the attention we get so we can control the reaction. This insecurity is how we complicate things for ourselves.

Simple living comes easy when we see no reason to cling, collect or hoard as if we're not safe. Our safety cannot be threatened so we don't need to build walls of defense.

Simplifying is trashing that type of anxiety and worry. Trashing the facades, pretenses and fake identities we create in order to belong. When we understand there's nothing we need to belong to, there's no need to force fit into what exists only to protect our insecurities. We are extensions of all that is—the universe, God. We already belong.

What This Feels Like

Simplicity feels like flow. It feels like spaciousness to move, shift and change—not just in our surroundings, but in our minds. It feels like choosing ease over effort.

Simplicity feels like the freedom to move around, to pick up and move to another country. It feels like the ease of throwing out the things that don't serve you anymore. It's effortlessly cleaning house, donating old toys, throwing out the stuff that doesn't fit or is past its expiration date. We may know the feeling of sentimental attachment, but it doesn't paralyze us when we decide to get rid of what feels unnecessary.

Simplicity feels like going with the flow because we're not resisting and hoarding things to give us the illusion of comfort or safety. It feels like safety without all the stuff we used to collect in order to bolster our sense of identity and prestige. It feels like being happy with what you have, not coming from a place of lack.

A Tool for Simplifying

A good tool to start simplifying our minds is a daily calendar—for its schedule and time blocks. There's freedom in discipline, and disciplining your day toward priorities is important. When we have a set schedule of nonnegotiable tasks, we won't let anything interfere and we put our priorities first.

The calendar also helps us schedule days of cleaning. Spring cleaning, fall cleaning, etc., all these things can be done when they're actually scheduled in. It's typical that if we don't write them down in our calendar, we won't ever do them. And sometimes we have to force our priorities into our schedule. Our calendar reminds us that it's good to evaluate our day based on our priorities.

A calendar helps us be mindful about what we schedule into our days. We want to look at our day's agenda and feel peaceful knowing we chose what's in there. We want to know we can set a time and a place for everything (in both mind and environment).

There's an optimal time of day for certain activities. For example, I'm most creative in the mornings which means I'm best at writing and strategizing in the mornings. Then I will move tasks that need little creativity to the afternoons, like checking email and reading articles.

In the evenings, I find it easy to review the day's completed tasks and plan the next day.

Find your creative time blocks (typically when you have the least distractions). Find your cleaning time (maybe when you can blast your favorite song as you dust and mop). Find your meditation time (ideally when you can be still and alone). Make these non-negotiable appointments with yourself.

If you're time blocking these "appointments" into your calendar, you can set the timer for, say, 30 minutes. When that timer goes off, you stop. Hold yourself to a timeframe for each appointment and you'll start to get more done in less time because you have an entire day's schedule to respect. If you go over on one task, you creep into and compromise other tasks. Trust yourself to start and end on time.

On your calendar, leave some empty days to do nothing. Let these days be about leisure. Also schedule days of exploration. Let these days be about exploring you, exploring new things and venturing out of the ordinary into the unknown, like facing your fear of heights in a hot air balloon.

Experiment
Week 7

This week, focus on simplifying.

Your game plan for the next seven days:

1. Increase your sitting meditation this week by one minute, so you're sitting for a total of seven minutes each morning. Let your mantra be, "I live simply." Repeat it quietly to yourself, over and over during this time. When your mind wanders, return your attention to your mantra: **I live simply.**

2. Change up your routine. Your route to work. The meal you pack for lunch. The purse you use. Your exercise routine. Pick something new and different so you can enter with a beginner's mind. Go back to basics, those times when you were new to something and you were wide-eyed and curious. Begin again. Beginnings have a way of reminding us of our youthful innocence, that de-cluttered place. Being a novice is akin to simplicity because we

go into that new activity or new path and welcome its lessons, its differences, and we allow it to change us.

3. Change up the place where you work. If you're in an office building, go to a vacant office. If you work from home, take your laptop or notebook and go into a different room. Go work at Starbucks. Go work outside in the garden. Get into a new environment. Shake up where you go to be productive if you're finding that you keep getting distracted by the same routine or the mess on your desk. Wanting to clean the mess around your desk instead of starting to work on projects is a distraction. Wanting to check social media because that's what you always do when you sit down at your desk, is a distraction.

As you work in these different settings, watch your reaction. Are you telling yourself the other way is easier, that you're just complicating things by trying to find a new place to work? Don't let habit and monotony trump the opportunity to find joy and excitement in newness. Start with what feels easiest. Change rooms. Go sit outside. Your mind may have you convinced that you must stick to the same routine because that's the most productive, when in actuality, you're precluding yourself from refining your workflow. Test it out; see if it doesn't get your juices of creativity flowing more when you change your environment and allow a beginner's mind that's not inundated with habit or distraction to take over. Occupy your mind with newness so you can get back to work.

4. Start simplifying your schedule, your day, your week, your year by consciously looking to eliminate and remove things that aren't serving you or benefitting your peace of mind. There is only goodness that flows on this river of life and if something is blocking that goodness from moving your raft, then get rid of it. Thoughts, people, objects. If your attachment to that commitment or collection is carrying your raft off course, throw it overboard.

Your energy is agitated from the clutter you see around you, yes, but, ultimately, *you* distract yourself from getting things done. Having to "clean up first" is an excuse. It is a lie we tell ourselves because we're avoiding work because of insecurity. We're convinced that we need to organize, put stuff away and vacuum before we can be productive. Not true. You're distracting yourself from "success" and forward momentum by letting clutter distract you. Simplify your distractions to none this week. If you're working at home or in an office, go someplace new. See if you're able to get inspired by the change in your surroundings.

What excuses are you hiding behind to "explain" why you're procrastinating?

savor

Live in the sunshine, swim the sea, drink the wild air.
—RALPH WALDO EMERSON

To *savor* is to relish and delight in a Feeling. It's basking in the sensations of an experience. We savor moments when we sit in a Feeling, be it painful or pleasurable, notice its richness, its impermanence, and appreciate its coming and going. We don't need to change it; we just allow it to arise, and allow it to pass.

To savor is to appreciate. Savoring a situation with our senses is to take in an experience, gratefully noticing all the sounds, smells, sights, textures and flavors that accompany it.

Savoring is placing our attention on a situation fully, openly and fondly. When savoring the sensations of a situation, we embody the utmost Feeling of love. We are unconditionally loving the moment.

Savoring is what our six senses are for, to soak in the fullness of our experience. Marinate in your senses! Deliberately take in every sound, every scent, every sight, every texture, every flavor, and let it all penetrate your being. Reflect on the beauty, the simplicity, the power. Notice the trees, flowers, laughter, lovers, birth, death and your reflection. Let the Feeling alone linger. Let your ears really listen to the sweet song of a bird. Let your nose really smell the soft aroma of a rose. Let your eyes really see the gentle sway of a tree. Let your hands really feel the grainy texture of a rock. Let your mouth really taste the ripe freshness of a blueberry.

And then let it pass.

How It Clears Clutter

Savoring is taking in the moment and leaving out the clutter. Savoring is a beautiful thing, the way it makes us grow in awareness and appreciation of all our senses. It's really coming into witnessing our mind-body connection. Tuning into our senses, being with them, indulging in them, taking them in. It's letting the world meet us where we are, and us enjoying the encounter.

There's so much more to experience than our limited perspective can even comprehend. Our stories are our stories. They'll stay there until we find something else to believe. To each his own. But when we allow ourselves time to Feel each sense for what it offers to us in any moment, we are opening ourselves up to the freedom of enlightenment, where everything can be seen as beautiful, magical and enjoyable. We allow everything to be as it is, and we get to explore how it enlivens our senses and our human experience.

Yes, our sixth sense will want to think about and interpret all sensory messages because savoring involves thinking. Gratitude, respect and recognition, for instance, are mental processes (thought) that come up whenever we savor a moment. Yet, while we can't ever escape the mind (not that we want to), the first eight steps of the Code prepared us to access spirit-mind more frequently so we can consciously observe and absorb the pureness of our life experience without needing to label it, explain it, change it or criticize it.

When spirit-mind is front and center, ready to observe and appreciate, true savoring can take place. Meanwhile, body-mind, which is ready to control and manipulate, hangs out backstage. When savoring, we don't need to engineer or manufacture the moment so we feel better about ourselves. Our savoring welcomes the *now* as it shows up while we remain equanimous with whatever happens.

What This Feels Like

Savoring feels like presence. Savoring is actively and consciously feeling. It's conscious witnessing of Feeling. To savor anything means to really take it in with our senses, to really feel it. We savor moments, people and things all using our senses. We savor by absorbing the Feeling of an experience. While we savor, we're very much *in the moment*, present and aware of what we're experiencing.

To savor a moment is to deeply absorb the sensory experience that it instills in the body. It's to feel the situation in its entirety without condition or expectation. To welcome it as it is. It feels like open arms, open hearts, open minds, welcoming the moment completely, unconditionally, without needing it to be different than what it already is. If we resist what's currently happening in our environment, we are not savoring what is. We're attempting to change it and make it different in some way. Some more pleasing way. But by trying to change it, we aren't savoring it.

A Tool for Savoring

The body is our tool for this step. Using our six senses to take in the world involves using our body. Experience whatever offers a sensory encounter, and sit with that and feel that in the body. Be with it. Don't do anything about it, just soak it in.

I like to go out in nature, leaving magazines, books, my cell phone and music playlist behind. I take time in nature to center my mind, sink my feet into the earth, smell the flowers, and rub my hands along the tree trunks. Sometimes I grab fresh berries from the market and head to the park to complete my simple sensory experience with nature's sounds, smells, sights, tastes and textures all swaddling me. It's beautiful to connect with nature this way, because it's connecting with myself and what I'm made of. I find that the time spent in nature calms my mind. The fresh air oxygenates my blood. The sun and breeze relax my body. Tension falls away. I'm centered toward spirit energy and I feel free for those few minutes.

Thoughts of gratitude may pop in and out. Thoughts of what to do later, or who to bring with me next time pop in and out. Let all thoughts come, receive them gracefully, sit with them a moment, and then encourage them to go. If you're able to sit in nature to explore *savoring* in your body, see how many thoughts come up during that time, how frequently they change, and what they tend to be about. The past? The present? The future?

No need to try to control the thoughts, just observe. Be mindful of any tendency to fall into patterns of complaining, anxiety or fear when faced with any sensory perception. Are you able to grab hold of any of them? Are any of them about the trees you're looking at? The sky? Are you present enough to think about where you are now? Or are you off worrying about something that may never happen and doesn't affect this exact moment?

Experiment
Week 8

This week, savor every moment by lingering in the sensations. Laugh longer, cry harder, smile bigger—let yourself feel these sensations and how it affects your sense of peace.

Your game plan for the next seven days:

1. Increase your sitting meditation time in the morning by one minute, so your timer is set for at least eight minutes. Let your mantra be, "I savor every moment." Repeat it quietly to yourself, over and over during this time. When your mind wanders, return your attention to your mantra: **I savor every moment.**

2. Each morning this week, walk outside as soon as you can from the time you wake up, and stand out in the open patio or front porch and take three deep breaths of fresh air. If it's too cold to go outside, stand at an open front door to receive fresh air into your lungs, taking three big deep breaths. Count to ten as you inhale, and then hold for 2 seconds with lungs full. Then release, counting to ten as you exhale. Hold for 2 seconds with lungs empty before you begin the next round. Do it this way for the three rounds of breathing in and out.

3. Savor moments with friends and family this week. If you can't be together in person, get on the phone with them. If you must, time block the visits so you're not thinking about where else you have to be. Spend time with those who breathe life into you, those who empower you and those who keep you honest. Enjoy the togetherness, the laughter and the inside jokes. Cook dinner for mom and dad. Get on the floor with the kids and pull out crayons and a coloring book. Sneak away with your spouse to sip wine at the lake. Tap in to the feelings of compassion and gratitude that you feel for each person in your life. Breathe in every glance, every smile and every hug.

4. Take your time at every meal. Focus on mindfully eating, taking time to really taste your food. Indulge in different flavors like fish,

dark chocolate and pomegranate. If you're used to eating on the run or cramming food in your mouth, slow down. As you take a bite, chew each fork- or spoonful for at least 10 seconds, tasting the flavors, feeling the textures on your tongue. This week, avoid salt and hot sauce on your food so you can let the food's natural flavors shine. Try using only natural herbs and spices as the enhancer.

As you go about this week mindfully savoring, do you feel your senses heighten in sensitivity, almost as if they got a recharge? How does that enhance every meal, every song, every bath, every sunset? How can you maintain this level of awareness?

9

sort

To attain knowledge, add things every day.
To attain wisdom, remove things every day.

–LAO TZU

To *sort* is to categorize and arrange, and to clear away what doesn't belong. While the act of sorting may seem largely an environmental task, sorting itself is a mental function. Sorting means evaluating necessary from unnecessary. Truth from untruth. Form from Feeling. Sorting through what separates *you* from the *True You*. Seeing the you that sits as witness and embodying that perspective more and more—sorting consciousness from unconsciousness.

Sorting looks like sorting our way through negative and positive moods. Good and bad memories. Productive and unproductive thoughts. Once sorted, that which doesn't belong or have a place in our lives anymore can get removed.

Sorting helps us recognize and remove that which doesn't serve our highest good. When you uncover what's not serving you, the best thing to do is to let it fall away through your conscious decision. Choose to sort what separates you from people, from peace, from the life you want to live. Choose to clear the clutter that stands in the way.

How It Clears Clutter

Sorting is clearing a cluttered mind. Sorting is releasing the burden and pressure of clutter—the expectations, the demands. When we sort, we release the need to control and manipulate because that behavior isn't serving a return to peace. It does the opposite and causes blame, anxiety and perfectionism. If one of the symptoms of clutter is seeking to control the external world, sorting is discovering what we do and do not have control over. We do not have control over the rocks that hit our raft, the ripples that threaten to tip us over, the sun that burns our skin, or the other rafters along the way.

Sort through your environment in people, places, possessions and priorities and determine what doesn't fit in your ideal life. What's holding you back from fulfillment and joy? Because everything is infused with energy (everything *is* energy), if there's an energy of anxiety around a subject or object, your thoughts about that are infecting and affecting your environment with anxious energy. If you notice your energy drains whenever you're around a certain person, in a certain room of the house or holding a certain object, then your thoughts about that person, room or object are stealing your peace. So sort it out, isolate and assess its energy with mindful presence and awareness, and either trash it or change your thoughts about it. That's in your power to do. On the other hand, if you notice that your energy improves around a certain person, in a certain room, holding a certain object, then the thoughts about those things serve an overarching idea of peace for you. Go with that.

It's all energetically, and psychologically, connected.

What This Feels Like

When we sort through things in our lives—be they people, memories or objects—we can feel our way to a decision. Sorting in this way is letting Feeling be our guide. We allow Feeling to tell us when we need or don't need something by the way it makes us feel when we hold it or examine it. We look at the person, place or thing and decide which of them inspires feelings of peace, ease, joy, love and Truth. Depending on how you want to feel, Feeling lets us know what can stay and what can go.

If you fear you might regret a decision to let something go, look back at someone or something you've let go, and how would you label your Feelings about the loss? Relief? Regret? Where does the sensation vibrate in your body? That vibration points to the origin of pain, which is not directly tied to that person or object. There's something deeper assigning your label. And it dates back to before that person or object arrived in your life. Sit with the Feeling without the label to get to the core pain. This will help you realize it had nothing to do with any*one* else or any*thing* else; it was always you and your interpretations. You might still be sitting with that pain moving forward in your life because you never made room for the insight until now. Now you can be free from the pain of regret because you've sorted through the misperception and let that go, too.

Ultimately, sorting feels like releasing the burden of clutter, releasing the weight and pressure of it. Sorting frees us from the hangups, the headtrash and the habits that keep us down. We sort through the fog and find clarity.

A Tool for Sorting

A tool for sorting is a trash bag! The symbolism of a trash bag is that we can get rid of anything that doesn't fit into our lives anymore. By now, we've opened ourselves up to new perspectives and maybe things we used to hold onto don't serve us or make us excited anymore. The burden of junk, unforgiveness and angst is trash. Get rid of it. Tie it up in your mind's trash bag and throw it out. Get rid of anything you don't love or need in mind, body, heart and home. Toss it out without a second thought. The reason we held on for so long is just an illusion anyway. Every day, seek to trash the burdens that zap energy from your life. Find renewal often.

When I go to clean up a room in my house, I naturally grab a trash bag and eagerly start filling it up. Papers, mementos, pens with dried ink and old socks get thrown out! It's something I do once a month and I shoot to fill the trash bag up within 15 minutes. A full trash bag is my simple aim. As I fill the bag, I notice what I'm *not* throwing inside and what stays in place on shelves, on tables and in drawers. What I keep starts to shine again in relevance because my mind simplified its desires and renewed its appreciation for the things I decided to keep.

Sort and release. After sorting your possessions and priorities, release what doesn't have a place or serve a purpose anymore. Free yourself from the load.

Experiment
Week 9

This week focus on sorting through what's working and not working in your life. Sorting comes easiest when we let Feeling lead, when we're tapped in to conscious awareness.

Your game plan for the next seven days:

1. Increase your sitting meditation by one minute this week, so every morning this week, you'll sit for at least nine minutes. Let your mantra be, "I sort and release." Repeat it quietly to yourself, over and over during these few minutes. When your mind wanders, return your attention to your mantra: **I sort and release.**

2. If you stopped journaling after Step 4, go back to journaling every day this week. This time, after you finish the day's entry, tear it out of your notebook and immediately throw it away—without delay or a second read. And throw away all seven of the journal entries from Week 4 (and any additional entries if you've continued to journal since).

    Physically free yourself from the words, the poetry, the burdened thoughts and whatever else you wrote by throwing it away and not giving it a second thought. However prolific the entry was, however profound and impactful, throw it out. Throw every page in the trash, even slide it through the shredder. Do not keep these. We're experimenting with sorting and detaching from that which we release. (If you plan on journaling after this week, you decide whether you save or discard your entries.)

3. Take a warm bath and light some candles. As you sit with your body submerged in the water, think about your life and all that you feel is working and not working so far. What do you want to let go of but you're scared to? Whatever it is, imagine it being pulled from your pores as you sit in the bath. The water, so cleansing, is extracting from you all the fear, anxiety, negative thoughts and limiting beliefs that hold you hostage.

    After ten minutes of drifting, release the stopper and visualize your "problems" circling down the drain with the bath water. Do this exercise as often as you'd like this week.

4. Sort through your belongings, searching for what doesn't serve you, and remove it from your life. Throw it in the trash bag! If it is an obstacle to peace, sort and remove it. Clothes, dishware, greeting cards, makeup, etc. Let every purge strengthen a clear path to consciousness.

Sort through what's not working for you and discard it. Pause and ask, "Is this working for me?" Yes? Keep it. No? Get rid of it! How easy is it for you to feel a clear Yes or a clear No when you ask that question?

10
sleep

Sleep is the best meditation.

—DALAI LAMA

Rest. Reset. Restart. Sleep, it's that weapon we all have to improve our mental functioning, our stamina and our muscular strength. It sustains the body's proper functioning, alertness and survivalism. During sleep, the body repairs bones and tissues, rejuvenates cells and organs. Sleep also boosts the immune system and aids digestion.

Sleep readies us for a new start. It is creating the time to break away from the hustle and bustle of life and give into the nothingness of being. It's choosing to retreat, to pull back from the kinetic and chaotic energy in the world. The mind relaxes. The nervous system relaxes. The postural muscles rest. The eyes rest.

Just as sitting meditation is a discipline, so is making enough time to mentally and physically shut off. We're not made to go nonstop 24/7; our bodies need time to rest. Too little sleep results in mental unrest, lethargy, poor memory and delayed comprehension. Sleep turns off access to the mind so the mind can process already learned information, readying it for interpretation and application—all of which eventually becomes the content of our dreams.

Sleep is non-doing. It gives us a break from the day-to-day grind of doing and moving. The mind rests from duties and tasks. The body moves into an inactive state. Both mind and body are able to rest for kinesthetic, emotional and psychological rejuvenation. Both are able to restore and ready themselves for the next several hours of waking life. We need rest as much as we need mental and physical activity.

How It Clears Clutter

Sleep helps facilitate decluttering. When we sleep, we consciously give into letting go. We allow ourselves to unplug from agendas, appointments and obligations that keep us so busy. As can be expected with hectic schedules and way too much mentally-taxing multi-tasking, our sleep patterns and quality of sleep are affected. Insomnia happens. We are essentially sacrificing sleep for *thinking about* sleep.

If at bedtime we're always worried about the day or about tomorrow, our precious time for sleep gets compromised because of poor planning. So instead of sleeping, we're thinking about how we're not working. We're sabotaging both rest *and* productivity. A vicious cycle.

Rest and productivity suffer from overthinking. Insomnia can be cured when we stop thinking about what we're *not* doing. When we stop worrying about what we lack. By ridding worry and thought-overload, we make space for adequate, refueling sleep. We calm the chaos and we declutter.

Sleep gives us time to reset. With a sufficient amount of sleep behind us, we make healthier decisions because we're not swayed by weariness. Destruction, despair and delirium exist in a restless mind and body.

When we're not mentally sharp, we don't make the best decisions for ourselves because we're disconnected from our Truth, from our ideal. We weaken. We start eating unhealthy foods and sweets. We start hanging with "the wrong crowd." We start getting sick more often. We start making hasty decisions in business and we lose money and momentum.

When we're mentally fatigued, it's difficult to steer clear of sabotaging habits like complaining, comparing and controlling. We can fall into hopeless thinking. Without enough rest, we impair our well-being out of sheer exhaustion.

What This Feels Like

Sleep feels like rest and relaxation. It feels like deliberately getting off our feet and falling into leisure. Where muscles are no longer working to keep us actively upright, but rather releasing the effort of stability and support. It feels like surrendering to shutting off. It feels like easing up, slowing down and letting go.

When we are sleepy, we feel slow, tired and lethargic. Being mentally-drained feels like exhaustion, while getting adequate sleep feels like alertness.

Sleep feels good! Sleep is revitalizing because it feels good to be rested and alert. There's a lightness in spirit and a bounce in our bodies after adequate sleep.

How good do you feel after a good night's rest? Imagine yourself on a Sunday morning after a deep sleep, waking up, sun peeking through the drapes, and you stretching your entire body as you slowly open your eyes. It's magical.

A Tool for Sleeping

A comfortable bed is your tool in this step. Sleep in it! At least seven to eight hours a night. If you're getting six, work up from there. Any less and you're really impacting your holistic health, despite what you think you can "live" on. Many of us don't get enough sleep; we're too preoccupied with seeking validation and approval, playing games on our phones, scrolling social media, writing to-do lists...all at bedtime. Yet we've all been taught that sleep keeps our bodies healthy and minds sharp. So why would we ever compromise that?

It's easy for me to fall asleep. As soon as I hit the pillow, I'm out within seconds. This is because, during a typical day, I meditate, journal and spend some time alone, so when it comes time to sleep, I've done enough to take care of my mind that it can easily shut off.

I also credit my ability to fall asleep fast to a bedroom environment where sleep is possible. The comfort of my bed matters to me. Otherwise, I'll be tossing and turning. The mattress has to be firm with an adequate amount of softness like from memory foam or a pillow top. If it's taking you long to fall asleep, a better mattress might help the situation. Create your comfortable sleeping environment. Set the temperature just right. Get the room really dark and quiet. (As for my bedroom, I like to keep the blinds open during the summer so I naturally wake up with the sunrise.)

Diet is important for a good night's sleep as well. I don't eat or drink alcohol less than two hours before going to bed. If I do, the continuity of my sleep suffers. And chances are I'll be wide awake in the middle of the night.

Take a 20-minute power nap during the day; it's the perfect amount of time to reboot. This is something I do whenever I can. Around mid-day, our minds and bodies have worked a lot, especially if you were in creation-mode in the morning hours like I am—working on projects that require complete focus and imagination. And after lunch, our bodies slow dramatically. So a quick nap might be a welcomed respite to encourage more waking hours of alertness.

Experiment
Week 10

This week focus on rest. We don't always give ourselves the rest we need, but this week, make it a priority.

Your game plan for the next seven days:

1. Increase your sitting meditation by one minute so you're at a total of ten minutes every morning this week. Let your mantra be, "My mind and body are well-rested." Repeat it quietly to yourself, over and over during this time. When your mind wanders, return your attention to your mantra: **My mind and body are well-rested.**

2. Take a cold shower right before bed every night this week. Let the cooler temperature in the shower facilitate improved circulation in the body. Studies show that a cold shower relieves stress, clears blocked arteries and boosts immunity. After you finish your shower, quickly get into a warm bed. Make adjustments to the temperature in the room to allow for a comfortable and cozy night's rest.

   In the morning, let's continue to take advantage of the nourishing benefits of water. Immediately upon waking, hydrate. Drink one half liter of filtered, lukewarm water to get your organs flushed out and joints lubricated. Add nothing to the water, keep it pure. Wait 30 minutes from your last gulp before eating.

3. Before you crawl into bed, grab a pen and a notepad—maybe a set dedicated to this activity alone that stays in your nightstand—and write down everything you'd like to get done tomorrow. Keep the list feasible. Be sure to gauge if you have enough time to get it all done without overtaxing yourself. Go into writing your list with the intention: if I only got these things done tomorrow, it would have been a

productive day. For the sake of time, stay general and brief, like, 1.) write a blog post, 2.) bathe the dogs, 3.) do laundry, 4.) meet Vanessa for Happy Hour. Once complete, put the notepad back in your nightstand. Go to bed with a clear head, knowing what needs to get done will get done tomorrow. In the morning, after you've taken time to hydrate, meditate, exercise and shower, review your list. Begin your day mentally ready to tackle it all.

4. Just as you would make time to work on your projects, time block your sleep. Time block between seven and eight hours of sleep each night this week. If you want to wake up at 6:00 am, count backwards seven or eight hours to arrive at your bedtime, 10:00 pm. Write it in your calendar and set your alarm to alert you when pajamas should be on and you should be in bed, your body lying on the mattress. Adjust what you need to adjust in your schedule to make accommodations for this timeframe. When your alarm for bed goes off, go to bed! Without TV, books, cell phones, etc. Just you, the dark, and your pillow.

To assist you in falling asleep, lie down and recap the day, starting from bedtime and working backward to when you woke up. Rehash every activity through the evening ("...went to bed at 10:00 pm, took a cold shower, brushed my teeth, drank tea, read an article, watched TV for an hour, ate grilled chicken and salad for dinner...") all the way through the morning ("...ran on the treadmill, brushed my teeth, meditated, drank one half liter of water, woke up to my alarm."). Silently recap everything you remember doing. I read this advice in a book years ago (the title escapes me now) and it always does the trick when my mind is racing 100 mph and I can't seem to settle. By the time I get to late afternoon, I'm knocked out!

Most importantly, when bedtime comes, get into bed. Leave your phone far enough away so you have to get out of bed to grab it when the alarm goes off in the morning. This way you're not tempted to text or pass time on social media waiting to get sleepy.

Ready your bedroom for a comfortable night's sleep. Learn your own physiology and the effect of eight hours of sleep on your body versus seven hours, six hours, five hours. Which feels the best? Can you adjust your schedule and bedtime accordingly?

CHAPTER 14

THE MENTAL WRAP-UP

How do you feel? You've just made it through ten weeks of decluttering! Congratulations. If you did the work, my guess is that you're feeling a lot less burdened by clutter than before you began the process.

Repeat the steps and experiments of the Declutter Code as often as you'd like. If you want to extend one week's experiment to two weeks, do it! It will make the results that much more profound. If you feel you could use more awareness in any one area, spend some more time on that step. This is your journey. Make the steps yours.

The inner game of life can be won by simply slowing down, stilling the mind, silencing the noise, and observing (seeing) the space between thought and reaction. We can shift our perspective whenever we decide to, and we can decide to give and receive compassion and love at any time. We simplify our lives to savor precious little moments. We sort between joy and misery and we keep around that which feels peaceful and allows us a good night's sleep.

Whenever you think you don't have the patience or the time to practice the Code, simply close your eyes and state the steps in order out loud to yourself. On every inhale and exhale, say a step and feel it throughout your body. Embody the word and its association.

It will go like this:

"Slow," inhale.
"Still," exhale.
"Silence," inhale.
"Space," exhale.
"See," inhale.
"Shift," exhale.
"Simplify," inhale.
"Savor," exhale.
"Sort," inhale.
"Sleep," exhale.

You will have completed five deep and slow breath cycles and should feel composure restored. If not, repeat it, taking in another five breaths. This alone does wonders to calm any nervousness or tension in your body and mind. That might be all you need in that moment.

Interesting, isn't it, how we have to use the power of the mind to restore the power of the mind? In all the ten steps, that's what we're doing. We use thought to perceive the mind's innate power. So it's important that we take care of the mind, foster its awareness and feed it positive nutrients like adequate amounts of stillness, silence and sleep. Once we remember our innate power, we remember that we're safe and that our Feelings always guide us to clarity and peace.

THE GOAL OF DECLUTTERING

> 66
>
> *What we're seeing out there is the projection of where we're at—the projection of the clingings of our minds.*
> —RAM DASS

Like the analogy in Chapter 12, the process of decluttering is the same for the mind as it is for the house. The same for the house as for the heart. The same for the heart as for the body. The same for the body as for the office. And so on.

The goal of decluttering a space (including headspace) is clarity and peace. It's with clarity and peace that we can move about with ease, excitement and freedom. We return to a state of innocence and presence, free from the burdens of stigma, dogma and drama that don't serve the authenticity of who we are. Those *-mas*, that bit of clutter, diminish, attack and destroy who we are because we don't recognize the damage quickly enough.

Ultimately, clutter shows up as struggle, suffering, stress, self-sabotage and separateness because we're holding energy hostage, collecting it to create an identity for ourselves, hoarding it for comfort and security, suffocating our own freedom in the process. With the Declutter Code, we aim to declutter our lives and release the stories that have us living in lies, lack and limitation.

As the mind clears, the eyes see more, the ears hear more, the nose smells more, the skin feels more, and the mouth tastes more…purely.

We will always have clutter, sure, because thought is clutter, but we can begin to see through the clutter and let go of whatever disconnects us from our power supply. Once decluttered, there will still be thoughts, but they'll be different thoughts, no longer of sabotage, fear or insecurity. And there will be more pauses in place of chaotic, incessant chatter.

The outcome of clearing clutter is freedom. Imagine not being ruled by labels or definitions, free to respond according to Feeling. Imagine not hiding behind a persona that constantly changes according to the validation and approval from others. Imagine being free to be.

Decluttering clears away the virus of clutter that seeks to overpower that which is purely *us*. Decluttering connects us back to Source, where we have access to all we need, when we need it.

After moving through the ten steps of the Declutter Code, we are more tuned into our True Self—that enlightened and free-flowing being.

Clutter, both mental and environmental, will naturally fall away as quickly as you grow aware of it. It can't stick around. Awareness shines a light so bright that clutter won't have a place to hide. You'll witness the clutter in mind, body, heart and home start to diminish as soon as you place your intention and attention on letting it fall away.

Clarity awaits.

To get more clarity and more support, and to register for the online course where I guide you step-by-step through the Declutter Code, visit decluttercode.com.

ACKNOWLEDGEMENTS

My heart is full of gratitude. This was a labor of love and so many contributed to its completion, in the way of support, editing, marketing advice and more. The following helped this book become a reality. Thank you.

Dolores Santana, because you inspire an eloquent use of words.

Stephen Bowlin, because you always have my back as I chase my dreams.

Angela, Steve, David and Tamara, for being the best housemates any sister could ask for.

June Baterina. Where would I be without my bestie?

Cecil J. Ojeda. My own personal cheering section every step of the way.

Natalie Vartanian, Juliana Todorova and Melissa Steele, for your beautiful perspectives.

Rochelle Deans, for your shrewd eye.

To everyone else who supported me virtually and in person, you made the journey so rewarding.

INSPIRATION

In the spirit of gratitude, these incredible books helped inform my path of decluttering:

Chodron, Pema. *How to Meditate: A Practical Guide to Making Friends with Your Mind*. New York: Sounds True, 2013.

Keller, Gary. *The One Thing: The Surprisingly Simple Truth Behind Extraordinary Results*. London: Hachette Book Group, 2013.

Singer, Michael. *The Untethered Soul: The Journey Beyond Yourself*. Oakland, CA: New Harbinger Publications, 2007.

Taubman, Steve. *Unhypnosis: How to Wake Up, Start Over, and Create the Life You're Meant to Live*. San Francisco, CA: Powertrack Publications, 2005.

Tolle, Eckhart. *The Power of Now: A Guide to Spiritual Enlightenment*. Novato, California: New World Library, 1999.

Williamson, Marianne. *A Return to Love: Reflections on the Principles of a Course in Miracles*. New York: Harper Collins, 1992

ABOUT THE AUTHOR

Yvette Bowlin has always been a student of the mind. It started with her undergraduate and Master's work in Consumer Behavior and led to her studies of enlightenment and spirituality. Years of research and self-inquiry sent her down the path of discovering the root of our "clutter problem." Her work has been featured on Huffington Post, Los Angeles Business Journal, podcast interviews and more.

From observing anxiety in herself and others, Bowlin has pinpointed the reasons most people keep themselves stuck in sabotage, suffering, struggle and stress. But we don't have to stay stuck! Clutter stands in the way of peace, presence and clarity.

Bowlin learned the 'art of hoarding' early on in childhood and has since been meticulous about decluttering her life. She's created a simple process for doing just that, outlined in the ten steps of the Declutter Code. The underlying premise of her book, seminars and speeches is that the most effective way to declutter is from the inside out—starting with the mind.

Also a certified yoga instructor, Bowlin loves to help others come into mind-body awareness to better facilitate deep decluttering. Learn more about her at decluttercode.com.

Printed in Great Britain
by Amazon